# VALUES IN THE KEY OF LIFE:
## Making Harmony in the Human Community

*by*
### *Kent Koppelman*

Baywood Publishing Company, Inc.
AMITYVILLE, NEW YORK

Library of Congress Catalog Number: 00-037932
ISBN: 0-89503-217-1 (cloth)


**Library of Congress Cataloging-in-Publication Data**

Koppelman, Kent L.
    Values in the key of life : making harmony in the human community / by Kent Koppelman.
        p. cm.
    Includes bibliographical references and index.
    ISBN 0-89503-217-1
    1. Values--Psychological aspects--Congresses. 2. Values--Psychological aspects. I.
    Title.

BF778.K67  2000
170--dc21                                                                00-037932

Cover photo: *Starry Night* by Vincent Van Gogh used by permission AGE fotostock/Superstock

Cover design by Janet Koppelman

Photo of Kent Koppelman on back cover by Roger Grant

Other books by Kent Koppelman:

*The Fall of a Sparrow: Of Death and Dreams and Healing* (1994)
    Baywood Publishing Company, Inc., Amityville, NY.

A previous version of the essay "Was Orwell Wrong?" appeared in the *English Journal, 73*:2, published by the National Council of Teachers of English, p. 48, February 1984.

A previous version of the essay "In the Land of Liberty" appeared in *Religion & Public Education, 12*:1 & 2, published by the National Council on Religion and Public Education, p. 37, Winter/Spring 1985.

# DEDICATION

*This book is gratefully dedicated to*

**David Witmer**

*Who lived his life joyously*
 *even when he was dying;*
*Who spent his time reading these pages*
 *when he had little time left.*

*If you look hard you might find his face*
 *looking out between the words you read*
 *or as you turn the pages of this book . . .*

*and he'll be smiling.*

# Acknowledgments

Many people graciously gave the gift of their time and talent to read and respond to the essays contained in this book. None of them are responsible for the errors which remain, but all of them contributed to the clarity and coherence of the language used to tell the stories and express the ideas. First and foremost I want to say to Doris Witmer how deeply I appreciated her husband's help. I benefited greatly from David's detailed comments, wise suggestions, and from his enthusiasm. David liked what I was writing, and no matter how many revisions he suggested, he always encouraged me to continue. I only wish he could be here so we could celebrate the publication of this book together. I want to thank my wife, Jan Koppelman, for her reactions to various drafts of various essays in various stages of completion. Her advice and encouragement were essential for sustaining my efforts to complete this book. In addition, I want to thank those students, colleagues, and friends who read at least one draft of these essays and provided me with suggestions for revision. If I have forgotten anyone, I hope you understand that it was not intentional. Whenever I would receive suggestions for revising my essays, I would write a note to myself on a scrap of paper to indicate the person who had sent the suggestions, but when I began to collect these notes so I could express my gratitude to the many people who had helped me, I wasn't sure I had found all of the notes I had written. Having said that, I want to thank the following people for their many suggestions and their support: Donna Alecksen, Burt Altman, Terry Beck, Barb Chaney, Larry Cozad, Charlotte Erickson, Teri Faulkner, Craig Fiedler, Harry Gardner, Lee Goodhart, Dan Green, Jean Hamons, Paul Heckman, Hal Hiebert, Tom Hood, Marcia Johnson-Sage, Robert Krajewski, Mary Newgard-Larson, Brent Larson, Jim Lewicki, Fran Luther, John Magerus, Ken Maly, Donald Marshall, Mick Miyamoto, Cheryl Niedzwiecki, Gen O'Grady, Joel Oines, Simcha Prombaum, Robert Richardson, Stuart Robertshaw, Karen Schoenfeld, Sonja Schrag, Ron Shaheed, Sara Slayton, Grant Smith, Greg Wegner, Ray Wilson, Janet Wollam, and Marty Zanger.

# Foreword

Teaching is the greatest form of optimism.
*Colleen Wilcox*

I am a teacher. In my classes I ask students to explain values as individuals and as members of a particular democratic society. I provide information and ideas about the forces and events that challenge our most deeply held values, issues stemming from differences such as gender, race, social class, disabilities, and sexual orientation. Although the subject matter is rarely pleasant, students recognize the significance of the issues and the need to understand them if we want to address them effectively as individuals and as a society. Despite the confusion and disappointments and the tragedies that continue to be part of the moral landscape in our society, I persist in my teaching in the hope that we can do better.

I thought about writing this book during the 1980s as conservatives marched onto the values battlefield and declared the territory their own. They were successful. The loudest voices demanding to be heard came from their camp. Although I respected many of these voices, I seldom agreed with them. I wrote two essays on values at that time and I was encouraged by their publication in professional journals, but before I could proceed, a personal tragedy interrupted my efforts.

My son was killed in an automobile accident at the age of nineteen. My grief disrupted all other plans and priorities and demanded attention. This lead me to write a book entitled *The Fall of a Sparrow: Of Death and Dreams and Healing* published in 1994. Although my grief did not end with the book's publication, it had been acknowledged and attended to, and that allowed me to renew my interest in writing this book of essays. One insight gained from writing *Sparrow* was my realization of the role of stories in coping with emotional pain and suffering. I began to use personal stories as a basis for the essays I wrote for this book.

The original idea for the book was to write a series of essays on values. In addition, I have collected quotations and anecdotes for the past twenty years and I hoped to include some of them in the book as well, but I was not certain how to do that. During one particularly sleepless night, the structure of the book came to me as the grandfather clock struck twelve times. I got out of bed and walked to the next room. I sat at my desk and wrote down the idea exactly as it had come to me. Here is a slightly revised version of what I wrote:

> *Identify the values which should be given the highest priority and devote a chapter to each one. Begin each chapter with an anecdote because stories are a useful starting point for expressing ideas. The anecdote is followed by a brief essay defining the value and contrasting it with a competitive value, meaning an attractive value that is difficult to reconcile with the other. Next, a section called "Hearing Voices" will consist of several quotations from people who lived prior to the twentieth century. Whether or not I agree with them, these quotations create a context for my own writing. After these quotations the first essay examines some aspect of the value which is the focus of that chapter. This is followed by a section entitled "Echoes" containing quotations from people living in the twentieth century to provide a contemporary context. Conclude each chapter with an essay where I examine another aspect of this value.*

As I continued to write and reflect on the values I had identified and was addressing in these essays, I realized that all seven of them had something in common: they were values that must be embraced if people want to develop the kind of relationship with others which can become the foundation for creating a sense of community. The Postlude essay provides the explanation for this conclusion.

The essays in this book are grounded in real events because values should not be regarded as abstractions but as the substance of our lives. Human beings try to define themselves according to the specific values which they believe are meaningful, but they are successful only when they demonstrate those values consistently in their actions. It is not easy. This book is for anyone who is engaged in the important and ongoing struggle to identify and practice those values which are meaningful to them not just as individuals, but as members of a community and as citizens of a multicultural, democratic society.

*Kent Koppelman*

# Contents

## Prelude

## Programme

# Postlude

ᖡ    ᖡ    ᖡ

# Preface

Knowledge alone is not enough, but our use of knowledge can make a difference. It is in the doing that knowledge becomes powerful. The same is true for the values described in this book. They are reflected in behaviors as we respond to ourselves and others in everyday life as well as in our professional work. How much have we thought about the values and beliefs that guide our lives, that support or limit us in being caring and competent adults whose behaviors support social justice?

Values lead to debates about whose role it is to teach or instill them in the young. They are learned from families, friends, teachers, religious leaders, heroines/heroes, and the characters on the little screens in our homes and the big screens in theaters. We expect teachers, youth workers, professional athletes, and others to reflect the values that students should emulate. We blame parents or schools when students "misbehave," often suggesting that the problem is the lack of appropriate values to guide their actions. And yet, we seldom talk about those values in classrooms or professional settings.

Kent Koppelman has broken that taboo in this book. At times his presentation has a religious basis, but the characteristics that he describes are applicable across religious beliefs and for non-believers as well. It is a courageous step to force us to think about our own values and their reflection in our personal and professional lives.

The personal stories throughout the book provide the means for surfacing discussions about values in the everyday. They force the reader to think about the personal. How would I have responded in a similar situation? Do my behaviors reflect my beliefs and values? The author appears to have internalized the values that comprise the book, and in most cases, his values guide his behavior. But there are times that he still has to think about the right thing to do, worried about possible personal danger in carrying out his values. We have all had times when it would have been easier to not act on our values, but they nag at us because we know "the right thing to do."

What is the relationship of these values and multicultural education? Knowledge and values are critical in understanding and delivering multicultural education. Multiculturalists seek information that helps them understand the world from multiple perspectives. They believe that there is no single history or superior literature or only one right way. They value diversity, equity, and social justice. The values that Kent Koppelman discusses in this book are among those that support multicultural education.

Many people espouse values, beliefs, and behaviors that respect differences and support social justice. Fewer people actually model these concepts in their own lives. We too often ignore racism, sexism, classism, and homophobia unless they directly affect us. We may serve the homeless on Thanksgiving, but forget them in the intervening 364 days. The struggle for most of us is to internalize the values that support multicultural education. With practice our personal commitment to these concepts and undergirding values become reflected in our everyday lives as we interact with others, confront inequity and discrimination, and work toward an equitable society.

What does it take to practice multiculturalism and social justice? A continuing thirst for knowledge beyond that with which we are familiar will expand our ability to examine events and issues based on their impact on persons with disabilities and from diverse racial, ethnic, language, and religious backgrounds. One of the best ways to know about differences and to overcome stereotypes and misinformation is to communicate and interact with persons from backgrounds and with experiences different than our own. We can learn by reading articles and books by others. We can hear and see the stories of others on the screen, but we often have to consciously seek the voice of others because we have become so comfortable with those we know best. The Internet may help us cross personal and cultural borders. We should not allow our knowledge and experiences to be limited by the place in which we live.

Kent Koppelman says that "we need to understand the problems and struggles of others outside of our most intimate group and have a similar regard for their lives." After we understand, we should support action that promotes social justice. Commitment to social justice requires more than service a few days a year. How could we insist that children and youth in our community have the best teachers and schools, and yet tolerate unlicensed teachers and dangerous conditions in the schools attended by other people's children? The sense of community and well-being has become parochial for many of us. We have not heeded the words of the author that call for us "to envision community on several levels, not just one's neighborhood, city, or state, but as a national and global enterprise . . . Only by supporting the freedom of others can we be assured of maintaining freedom for ourselves."

This book provides an insight into one advocate's philosophy and history translated to action in everyday living. Hopefully, it will be an inspiration to the rest of us to live our convictions and develop a multiculturalist vision that includes more than our own families and communities.

*Donna M. Gollnick, President*
*National Association for Multicultural Education*
*also Senior Vice President*
*National Council for Accreditation of Teacher Education*

# Prelude

*We have come a long road up from the darkness, and it well may be—so brief, even so, is the human story—that viewed in the light of history, we are still uncouth barbarians.*

Loren Eiseley, *The Firmament of Time*, p. 146, Atheneum, New York, 1966.

# Talk Radio

**Host:** Hello everyone! Bob Jones coming to you once again with a program of the people, by the people, and for the people because it gives people a chance to "Talk to me!" It's good to be in God's Country on the banks of the Mississippi, and let me say how especially good I feel being here tonight with Christmas just around the corner. This is my favorite time of the year and I'm sure that's true for most of my listeners out there. But speaking of listeners, let's get right to your phone calls. Hello caller, you're on the air. Talk to me!

**Caller:** Bob? Hello?

**Host:** Yes caller, I hear you. Talk to me!

**Caller:** My name is Hank Tucker and I just want to say . . . by the way I agree with you about Christmas but that's not why I called. I've been thinking about something and I'd like to get if off my chest.

**Host:** Go ahead, that's why we're on the air. Talk to me!

**Caller:** Well, actually I can relate it to Christmas because Christmas is about giving, and that reminds me of how generous our government is, and the people who benefit the most from this generosity are those people on welfare. Now here's my question—why doesn't anybody ask what they will give? With them it's always take, take, take.

**Host:** That's a good point, Hank. Everyone should have to give something back to this great country. Of course, some people will say that a lot of the money spent on welfare goes to children, and they have to grow up first before we can expect them to give some back.

**Caller:** I know. I know. People are always talking about the kids on welfare. Fine! But some of them are old enough to work, so what I want to know is—why aren't they working? I had a job when I was a kid, what's wrong with them? They're lazy, that's

3

|        | |
|--------|---|
|        | the problem. When my dad was growing up kids worked hard! They put in twelve, thirteen, fourteen hours a day in the factories or in the mines or on the farm. |
| Host: | You're absolutely right, Hank. Kids had it a lot tougher in the old days. |
| Caller: | You better believe they were tough! They had to be! Not these marshmallows today! Those were the days when people knew how to work. It's a dog-eat-dog world out there and it's never too early for even a kid to find that out. |
| Host: | Of course the people on welfare aren't all children, there's the mothers . . . |
| Caller: | Right! Now that's another story. These women on welfare say they can't work because they have to stay home and take care of their kids, but don't these kids go to school? And when they're not in school they ought to be working! There is no excuse for these lazy women to be sittin' around the house watching soap operas and reading *Cosmopolitan*. Make 'em work! |
| Host: | What about if they have young children, Hank? You know, babies or toddlers. |
| Caller: | Take the little ones to Grandma or leave 'em with a neighbor. That's really not any of my business. I didn't bring 'em into the world! If you can't afford to take care of your kids you shouldn't be havin' kids. And I sure as hell shouldn't have to be the one who has to take care of 'em! |
| Host: | I appreciate what you're saying, Hank, and I bet a lot of people share your frustration about these mothers having kids when they can't afford to take care of them. That's why we had to reform the welfare system and now we'll have to wait and see if the reforms work. I know a lot of my listeners are concerned about how the government uses their hard earned tax dollars. The government shouldn't be wasting that money. |
| Caller: | Talk about taking our hard earned money! Let's talk about retired people! The worst thing we did in this country was to have mandatory retirement, and the second worst thing was to start this Social Security. You know, some people say President Roosevelt was influenced by the communists, and for all I know he might've been. He had an awful lot of meetings with old Joe Stalin. Who knows what they were talking about! |
| Host: | It would be pretty hard to prove that FDR was a communist, but since you brought it up, I seem to recall that there were some people who accused Eleanor Roosevelt of having communist sympathies. |

Caller:   I can't say one way or the other, but I can tell you that Social Security took away the strongest incentive there is for old people to keep working—the fear that they would spend their savings and end up on the streets! I suppose that sounds a little harsh . . .

Host:   Well, yes it does, and I doubt that many of our listeners would agree with you on that.

Caller:   I don't care if they agree or not; it's still true isn't it? The truth hurts sometimes.

Host:   But what are senior citizens supposed to do, Hank? If you work hard all your life and pay your taxes, shouldn't you have the right to retire at some point? Shouldn't you be able to live in some comfort during your "golden years?"

Caller:   Let me ask you this . . . what did old people do before there was Social Security?

Host:   Well, I suppose they had to keep working until they had saved enough money to retire, and I suppose some of them lived with one of their children or grandchildren.

Caller:   That's right, they took care of themselves or their families took care of them, that's what they did, and that's the way it should be. I'm no spring chicken myself, but I plan to keep working until I drop. I don't ask anyone to take care of me and I don't think anyone else should ask me to take care of them. Just because they call themselves "senior citizens," what right do they have to ask me and other taxpayers to help pay for their food and shelter and doctor bills? Let 'em go out and earn the money to pay their own bills like everyone else has to do or get their children to pay for it, but don't ask total strangers to do it.

Host:   That's an interesting argument, Hank. It sounds like you want to dismantle all of FDR's social programs from the 1930s. You say you want to get rid of Social Security for the elderly and welfare payments for all those single women with children. Are you also opposed to the government supporting people who are blind or disabled?

Caller:   Yes I am. I'd like to get rid of *all* these government handouts. Handicapped people should stop whining and complaining and get a job. Now I know they can't do much, but they can do something! Hell, I've seen assembly line workers who just push a button or some such simple task. If a handicap don't have arms he could push a button with his toes couldn't he? What it all comes down to is what it says in the good book—those who don't work should starve! The Lord said that himself! You can look it up.

Host:     Well, I'm no expert but I think it does say something like that in the Bible.

Caller:   It sure does, and that reminds me, I was listening to some lady preacher on the radio the other day and she was talking about how we had to help poor people and I think she was quoting some guy, but I didn't catch his name. Anyway this guy said . . . now just let me think a bit . . . oh yeah, that if you've got two coats and someone else doesn't have a coat, then you should give him one of your coats or some such radical stuff like that. Just give it to him! She said you had to! Can you believe it?

Host:     I think I've heard that before . . .

Caller:   Well I don't know much about it and I certainly don't know who this guy is and I don't want to know him, but I would bet you the farm on one thing—I don't care who this guy is but he is no American!

Host:     I think you're absolutely right on that one.

Caller:   Just between you and me Bob, I think he's probably a communist. Anyway, that's all I have to say. It's been good talking to you, Bob. You know, I listen to you every day.

Host:     Thank you for calling, Hank. I always enjoy hearing from my listeners.

Caller:   Well I enjoy listening to your show, and since I'm on the air right now I'd like to say one more thing before I hang up.

Host:     Go ahead.

Caller:   Thanks Bob, I just want to say that I'm proud to be here in God's country, and I want to wish you and everyone listening out there a very Merry Christmas!

Host:     Thank you Hank, and a Merry Christmas to you, too. We have another phone call coming in. Hello, you're on the air. Talk to me!

Talk to me!

Talk to me . . .

talk to me . . .

## CROSS TALK

*One is what one believes*
> Anton Chekov

> *If we believe absurdities*
> *we shall commit atrocities.*
>> Voltaire

*We can believe what we choose.*
*We are answerable for what we*
*choose to believe.*
> Cardinal Newman

> *You may be sure that when one begins to*
> *call himself a "realist," he is preparing*
> *to do something he is secretly ashamed of*
> *doing.*
>> Sidney Harris

*People seem not to see that their*
*opinion of the world is also a*
*confession of character.*
> Ralph Waldo Emerson

> *It is the duty of youth to bring its fresh*
> *new powers to bear on social progress.*
> *Each generation of young people should*
> *be to the world like a vast reserve force*
> *to a tired army. They should lift the world*
> *forward. That is what they are for.*
>> Charlotte Perkins Gilman

*Seek not to know who said this or that,*
*but take note of what has been said.*
> Thomas a Kempis

> *Who shoots at the mid-day sun, though he*
> *be sure he shall never hit the mark; yet as*
> *sure he is he shall shoot higher than who*
> *aims but at a bush.*
>> Sir Philip Sidney

*Never doubt that a small group of
thoughtful, committed citizens can
change the world. Indeed it is the
only thing that ever has.*

Margaret Mead

*For each age is a dream that is dying,
Or one that is coming to birth.*

Arthur O'Shaughnessy

# Programme

*We must never accept utility as the sole
reason for education. If all knowledge is
of the outside, if none is turned inward,
if self-awareness fades into the blind
acquiescence of the mass man, then the
personal responsibility by which democracy
lives will fade also.*

Loren Eiseley, *The Firmament of Time,* p. 146,
Atheneum, New York, 1966.

# CHAPTER ONE
# In the Key of A:  ALTRUISM

## AT HEAVEN'S GATE
### ("*ianua caeli, ora pro nobis*")[1]

There was a rich old miser who died and was being interrogated at the Pearly Gates. St. Peter told the man that a brief examination of the Book of Good Deeds did not reveal that he had done enough good in his life to warrant entry into Heaven. "Wait a minute," said the sinner, "In 1913 I gave a blind man selling pencils a nickel and let him keep the pencil." St. Peter flipped through hundreds of pages until he finally found the entry. "Was there anything else?" "Well, in 1919 during a blizzard I gave a dime to a poor woman who was stranded and had no cab fare." St. Peter, after much searching, located the reference. "Still not enough," said the guardian of the Gate. "Don't send me to Hades yet," pleaded the old scrooge. "In the early 1930s, I was going by an orphanage and I saw an urchin with no shoes on and I gave him a quarter!" St. Peter checked and saw that this was true. "I still don't think you qualify, but we'll appeal your case to a higher authority." With that, St. Peter picked up the telephone. After an animated conversation, he hung up. "What did He say?" asked the anxious miser. "He says to give you back your forty cents and tell you to go to Hell" [1, pp. 134-135].

> **Altruism**—the principle or practice of unselfish concern for (or devotion to) the welfare of others

I have had discussions where any talk of altruism is brusquely dismissed and altruistic behavior is regarded as noble but unrealistic. The consistency of this reaction has puzzled me. It makes no sense to envision a concern for others as equivalent to *peace on earth* or *love everybody* or other ideals beyond the reach of mere mortals, and yet that is how altruism was being described. Professions such as nursing,

---

[1]"gate of heaven, pray for us" from the Catholic "Litany for Loretto."

teaching, social work, and other human services do not tend to pay attractive salaries and could not attract sufficient numbers of people to enter them if having concern for others was such a rare human quality.

This confusion about altruism is not confined to the United States, nor to the present. In a discussion with Confucius, the skeptic Tsai Wo sarcastically claimed that if someone came running up to say a man had fallen into a well, the altruistic person would jump in the well to rescue him. Confucius responded, "Even an altruist would first make certain there really was a man down the well!" [2, p. 163]. In time I began to understand the basis for the dismissive responses. To qualify as altruistic, many people insist that a person's behavior must illustrate a selflessness usually associated with saintly behavior. This perception makes it difficult to imagine altruism being practiced by more than a handful of people; therefore, it becomes irrelevant.

When Jesus said to share a coat with your neighbor if you have two coats and your neighbor has none, he didn't say you had to give the coat away (Luke 3:11). My view of altruism would suggest that the coat you share wouldn't even have to be the best coat because any coat is better than none in cold weather. A person could give a coat or simply loan one to a neighbor until the bad weather ended, but in the selfless version of altruism, the only truly altruistic act is to give the neighbor BOTH coats. Some people might not insist on this, yet they would still assume that an altruistic person would at least give the neighbor the better coat.

This common perception is a curious exaggeration of the dictionary definition which only speaks of *an unselfish concern for or devotion to the welfare of others,* suggesting that altruism is a desire to help others without asking for something in return. Altruism means helping others simply because you want to. It is not unrealistic to expect someone to be concerned for another person regardless of the possibility of compensation or reward. Most people have probably been the beneficiary of unsolicited assistance from another person at some time in their lives. For example, while driving through Minnesota one time my car engine began to lose power and I had to pull onto the shoulder. A man in a pickup truck stopped to see if he could help. After he determined what was wrong and fixed it, he said the repair was temporary and suggested that I take the car to a mechanic as soon as possible. When I opened the car door to tell my wife what was happening, our good Samaritan got in his pickup and drove away before I had a chance to thank him or to offer him some money to express my gratitude. Obviously he did not offer his help with any reward in mind.

I don't believe my experience was unusual. Altruistic actions occur every day, yet people still insist that the only behavior legitimately qualifying as altruistic is when the assistance someone gives to another involves some kind of loss or suffering for the helper. Altruism is transformed from having a concern for others to martyrdom.

What competing value would make a person less likely to practice altruism? Some would propose selfishness as an obvious contrast to altruism, but in order for an alternate value to be meaningful it must appeal to people. Except for Ayn Rand, few people have argued for the virtue of selfishness. Ambition is a more reasonable choice. Ambition is a positive value which, if it were a priority, would make it unlikely for someone to behave altruistically.

> **Ambition**—an ardent desire for some type of achievement or distinction such as power, fame, wealth . . . synonyms include enterprising and aspiring.

In the United States, we promote the idea of being ambitious. We admire ambitious people because we see them as individuals likely to achieve their goals and attain some degree of status and wealth—the American Dream. We encourage our children to be ambitious and we criticize them if they display a lack of ambition. This value was even promoted by the U.S. government in the actions which were taken to address the "problem" of potlatch ceremonies.

In the northwestern United States, the Kwakiutl Indians lived and thrived in a culture which mandated that each household periodically host a potlatch ceremony. At the potlatch, the host would give away most of his possessions to those invited to attend. After soldiers seized their lands and forced the Kwakiutl onto a reservation, the U.S. government outlawed the potlatch ceremony. How were the Kwakiutl ever going to be successful if they kept giving away their material possessions? The potlatch tradition prevented the Kwakiutl from achieving the American Dream. This is why people are encouraged to be ambitious, so they will do everything they can to become prosperous. In our society, success is measured by one's possessions.

It should not be surprising that the U.S. government did not understand the complex role of the potlatch ceremony in the Kwakiutl culture, even the earliest ethnographers of the Kwakiutl did not fully understand it [3], but the consequences of one culture imposing itself on another was no different in this instance than in other occurrences. The sense of community among Kwakiutl people eroded with the disappearance of the potlatch ceremony, and the people suffered from a sense of disconnectedness from the other members of their tribe.

This cultural conflict illustrates the contrast between altruism and ambition. Ambition is self-serving. Ambitious people make decisions to advance their careers or contribute to their progress toward a goal.

Altruism responds to the needs of others. Altruistic people may feel good by helping others, but they do not do it for personal gain. It is possible to be ambitious and altruistic, especially when what is good for an individual is also good for others, but there will always be situations where one person benefits at the expense of someone else, or where an individual benefits at some cost to a group of people. The pattern of such choices an individual makes over a lifetime will determine which value has a higher priority.

The miser at heaven's gate argued that an occasional altruistic act involving a minimal charitable gesture defined him as a person worthy of heaven. His argument was not persuasive. Whether God is the judge or we are judging ourselves, the choices we make and the actions we take must constitute the basis for answering those fundamental questions: Who am I? What do I stand for?

### ❧ ❧ ❧
## HEARING VOICES

*Blessed is he that considereth the poor and needy: the Lord shall deliver him in the time of trouble.*

> Book of Common Prayer

*Man is God's image; but a poor man is Christ's stamp to boot.*

> George Herbert

*When people begin to ignore human dignity, it will not be long before they begin to ignore human rights.*

> G. K. Chesterton

*Birth, ancestry, and that which you yourself have not achieved can hardly be called your own.*

> Greek Proverb

*Wealth is a power usurped by the few to compel the many to labor for their benefit.*

> Percy Bysshe Shelley

*What has destroyed every previous*
*civilization has been the tendency to*
*the unequal distribution of wealth*
*and power.*

Henry George

*Our inequality materializes our upper*
*class, vulgarizes our middle class,*
*brutalizes our lower class.*

Matthew Arnold

*So our Lord God commonly gives riches*
*to those gross asses to whom He*
*vouchsafes nothing else.*

Martin Luther

*Behind every great fortune there is*
*a crime.*

Honore de Balzac

*The man who dies . . . rich dies*
*disgraced.*

Andrew Carnegie

*If you love yourself meanly, childishly,*
*timidly, even so shall you love your*
*neighbor.*

Maurice Maeterlinck

*The misfortunes of poverty carry with*
*them nothing harder to bear than that it*
*exposes men to ridicule.*

Juvenal

*The love of liberty is the love of others;*
*the love of power is the love of*
*ourselves.*

William Hazlitt

*Lord! We know what we are, but know*
*not what we may be.*

William Shakespeare

*Treat people as if they were what they*
*ought to be and you help them to become*
*what they are capable of becoming.*

Johanne Wolfgang von Goethe

*To be nameless in worthy deeds exceeds
an infamous history.*

Sir Thomas Browne

*The only reward of virtue is virtue; the
only way to have a friend is to be one.*

Ralph Waldo Emerson

*When we are planning for posterity,
we ought to remember that virtue is
not hereditary.*

Thomas Paine

*Poverty is a great enemy to human
happiness; it certainly destroys liberty,
and it makes some virtues impracticable
and others extremely difficult.*

Samuel Johnson

*I hold it for indisputable, that the first
duty of a state is to see that every child
born therein shall be well housed,
clothed, fed and educated, till it attain
years of discretion.*

John Ruskin

*Ideals are like stars: you will not succeed
in touching them with your hands, but
like the seafarer . . . you choose them as
your guides, and following them you
reach your destiny.*

Carl Schurz

## THE VALUE OF A DOLLAR

*to tithe*

*the tenth part of agricultural produce,*
*goods or personal income, is set apart as an*
*offering to God or for works of mercy . . .*

My father tithed. He was a truck driver earning a small salary. His primary income came from the commissions he earned selling animal feed to farmers. He worked six days a week driving his truck and on Saturday nights he would meet with farmers in the bars to socialize and to make more sales. Every Sunday morning he would calculate 10 percent of his commissions for that week, write out a check for that amount and put it in the church donation envelope. It was one way to thank God for His blessings and for the opportunity to have such a bountiful life. In the best economic year of his life my father earned perhaps $12,000.

I once saw a television documentary featuring interviews with successful people. One was an Amway dealer successful enough to have purchased an estate with a Tudor style mansion, a swimming pool, and a garage large enough to hold his five Rolls Royce automobiles. Apparently the value of a dollar for this man had to do with his ability to purchase housing and vehicles to announce his success. I was not impressed. I could only shake my head and say, "that man doesn't know the value of a dollar." I learned this value from my father.

Our local Chevrolet salesman was a Mason who once tried to persuade my father to join his lodge. Sensing some hesitancy, the salesman pressured my father with a "hard sell." He talked about how great it was to be a Mason because no matter where you were, you could always count on another Mason for help if you were in trouble. Seeing that my father was impressed with this argument, the salesman pursued the point with an illustration.

He described a business trip from a few years earlier. With no advance reservations, he was surprised to find that all the hotels in the city were filled. He tried everywhere but there was nothing available. The desk clerk at one hotel patiently listened as the salesman expressed his frustration and then he noticed the salesman's ring. The clerk asked if the salesman was a Mason. Hearing that he was, the desk clerk held up his right hand to show that he was wearing a Masonic ring. Although he had a family scheduled to arrive later, the clerk gave their room to his fellow Mason. He said he would apologize to the family for the error, and he would try to help them get a room somewhere else. The salesman concluded his story by saying how grateful he was to get a nice room and a good night's sleep. For him the story ended on a triumphant note, but it was a discordant note for his listener. The story convinced my father that he could never be a Mason. Most Masons would probably not endorse the salesman's story as exemplary of Masonic values, but my father was not pleased by what he had heard. He could not join an organization whose members boasted of such selfish behavior.

My father would not have slept well in that hotel room. He would have been too worried about the other family: How would they be able to find a room if all the hotels were full? How many children did they have? What did they do? The idea of joining a group to gain an advantage over the next person was not how my father perceived the value of a dollar. A dollar was not worth having if it came at the expense of others, if it caused suffering and misery to another human being. The value of a dollar was its power to provide for a pleasant life, and its potential for helping others.

It is never easy to talk about the value of a dollar in this way because cynics will take the argument to the extreme and then reject it. They will insist that people who make such an argument must take a vow of poverty and give away all their money and possessions, and if they do not they are denounced as hypocrites. I don't give away all my money nor do I say that others should. I think it is reasonable to do what my father did. He used the money he earned to create a comfortable life for his family. He could be frugal, buying used cars when new cars became too expensive, but he still spent a lot of money taking his family on trips. He saved for his old age so that he did not have to rely exclusively on Social Security. He encouraged and supported his children's dreams and helped pay for their college education. In addition to tithing at church, he also contributed regularly to orphanages and to other charitable organizations which helped people in need.

Although I try to model myself after my father, it has become increasingly frustrating in recent years to send contributions to charitable causes because so much of what is contributed appears to pay for the bureaucratic expenses of the organization, including fundraising costs. It is more satisfying to contribute to local groups where it is easier to ascertain how the money is spent. Perhaps most satisfying of all are the unanticipated opportunities to help another.

I was standing in line at a local K-Mart shortly after Christmas. The woman in front of me was a Southeast Asian immigrant who did not speak English. Her little boy, perhaps eight or nine years old, was her translator. The clerk had rung up all of her purchases but the money being offered by the woman did not cover the cost. With the boy's help, the clerk determined which items the woman definitely wanted to purchase and these were put into a shopping bag. With the remaining items they began negotiating which ones to set aside to get the total amount of the purchase low enough to be covered by the amount of money in the woman's hand. They were still five dollars short when the negotiations appeared to be stalled. The clerk at the cash register looked back and forth from mother to son, the mother looked at her son, but the little boy said nothing. Five dollars. I was beginning to feel irritated at the long delay.

Glancing at the items left on the counter, I noticed an action figure marked down to less than five dollars now that Christmas was over. Next to the toy were two household items which also cost about five dollars. If the toy were taken away, the mother would have enough money for the practical purchases. The mother was talking to the boy but he would not look at her. I pulled out my wallet and gave the clerk at the cash register a five dollar bill. The mother turned to thank me with a gracious smile and a slight bow of the head. I wished her a Merry Christmas.

I could not resist looking at the little boy. The troubled look on his face was transformed into a huge smile as the remaining items, including the toy, were put into the shopping bag. The pleasure that his reaction gave me was inexpressible. To see the look on his face and to know that I was responsible for it gave me a sense of satisfaction that no other five dollar purchase could give. I do not know if it is better to give than to receive, but in this case I felt more pleasure in giving a gift than I have ever felt in receiving one.

There is a footnote to this story. After mother and son left and I was paying for my own purchases, I noticed the woman next in line staring at me. As I turned to look at her she smiled and in a pleasant voice said, "Well, that was your good deed for the year." I was so startled I had to laugh and her brow wrinkled in confusion. I said, "For the *week*, perhaps." Her comment and the expression on her face implied that she could not fathom the pleasure I received from my gift to that little boy. She did not understand the value of a dollar.

Another example: A colleague told me about a woman in her early thirties who was enrolled in one of his college classes. He asked his students to keep a journal, and her entries revealed significant economic hardships: her husband was disabled and could not work; they had three children; the small government check he received each month was their main source of income. She was trying to complete her undergraduate degree so she could qualify for a teaching position and provide a better life for her family.

As Thanksgiving approached, he thought she seemed particularly despondent. One day after class he pulled her aside and asked if there was anything wrong. She was depressed because she did not have enough money to buy the food for her family's Thanksgiving dinner. They would have to eat at the community center. They had done this before. The free Thanksgiving dinner at the center was available to the less fortunate families in the community. With tears in her eyes, the woman said she simply wanted to make Thanksgiving dinner for her family.

My colleague had been invited by some friends to celebrate Thanksgiving with them. Since he would not have to buy a Thanksgiving dinner for his family, he wanted to buy the food for her family. When he suggested this she refused, but he insisted: "If I was not going to my friends for Thanksgiving I would have purchased the food for my family. I can certainly afford it. Since I have the money, let me have the pleasure of giving your family a Thanksgiving dinner." He persuaded her to accept his offer and they worked out the arrangements. On the day before Thanksgiving, he went to the supermarket and filled a shopping cart with turkey, cranberries, potatoes, and everything required for a traditional Thanksgiving meal. He took the bags of food to the woman's house and the next day he left town to visit his friends. After class the following week, the woman thanked him saying it was one of the best Thanksgivings her family ever had. He said that made it one of the best Thanksgivings for him as well.

There is also a footnote to this story. Just before Christmas this same student came to my colleague with a new dilemma. A cousin had been staying at her home for a week, but he had left suddenly and had stolen $5000 worth of jewelry from her. Aside from its monetary value, she said the jewelry was her only inheritance from her mother. When I first heard about this my first thought was to wonder if all the jewelry in my house was worth $5000. I doubted it. My colleague couldn't understand why she had come to him. Did she only want a sympathetic ear or did she expect more than that? He had mentioned this to his wife who said it was obvious that the woman was trying to play on his sympathy, hoping that he might offer her at least some of the money. His wife questioned the existence of the jewelry or the robbery, and she believed that his previous act of charity was the reason for this attempted "scam."

I asked if he thought his wife was right. He wasn't sure, and this troubled him. He always tried to think well of his students. Then I asked if this incident diminished the pleasure he felt from buying the food for the woman's family for Thanksgiving. His troubled look gave way to a smile and he responded immediately, "Not in the least." Even if she was lying about the theft of the jewelry, her poverty was real, and so was her anguish about not being able to make a Thanksgiving meal for her family. It was obvious that he felt as much pleasure remembering that he had made it possible for her to make a Thanksgiving dinner for her family as he did the day he bought the food.

I questioned how could he feel good about buying the food for a person who was possibly lying to him in an attempt to get money from him. He said there were "scams" initiated by wealthy individuals and multinational corporations which had cost other people hundreds of thousands of dollars. He said, "Why should poor people be any different? Where is it written that poor people have to be perfect? No one is perfect and neither am I, so who am I to judge the imperfections of others?" That was the end of the conversation, and he seemed content. The troubled look was gone. This was a man who knew the value of a dollar.

That our society has made judgments about which people are worthy of assistance is implicit in such phrases as "the deserving poor" or "the truly needy." These expressions suggest that only people who are good and decent should receive any kind of help, and our assistance should be withheld from poor people who are flawed in any way—people using drugs, people who are lazy, people who drink too much alcohol. But the most profound value of a dollar is in its power to redeem a human being. There are no guarantees. Happy endings are not automatic. When you give money to help another, it is important to take joy in the giving. Offering to help someone else is the equivalent of placing a bet, and the odds will vary from person to person. Some bets seem like a sure thing and perhaps they are; other bets seem risky but sometimes they may result in a dramatic success. Investing in people is a risk. Even when you win, your reward is likely to be emotional or spiritual rather than financial. You may see someone succeed and take pleasure in knowing you helped to make it happen.

There is value in a dollar that creates possibilities, opportunities, and hope. It might help the defeated stand up, open a door to those locked out, or lift the spirits of someone burdened by despair. It might, but it might not. Those who stand may fall again, others will not see the open door and some will be too weighted down to be lifted up. It is not the outcome that gives the dollar its value, it is the giving. The decision to gamble on a human life is what is important. The value of a dollar can be realized in large houses, luxury cars, and expensive jewelry, and this is the most common value it is given. The value of a dollar can also be expressed in terms of how it has nurtured human life and made it whole. When we affirm the redemptive value of a dollar, we pay it the greatest respect and assign it the highest value.

ã ã ã

## ECHOES

*The greatest of evils and the worst of crimes is poverty.*
George Bernard Shaw

*For every talent that poverty has stimulated it has blighted a hundred.*
John Gardner

*Love for one's country which is not part of one's love for humanity is not love, but idolatrous worship.*
Erich Fromm

*One of the signs of passing youth is the birth of a sense of fellowship with other human beings as we take our place among them.*
Virginia Woolf

*I firmly believe that mankind is so instinctively, unconsciously involved with the survival and growth of the species that when an individual attempts to live selfishly, he will either fail or fall into despair.*
Joyce Carol Oates

*No child should have to grow up on the streets. And every family should have a roof over its head.*
George Bush

*Real education should educate us out of self into something far finer; into a selflessness which links us with all humanity.*
Lady Nancy Astor

*A child miseducated is a child lost.*
John F. Kennedy

*The individual who holds that every
human right is secondary to his
profit must now give way to the
advocate of human welfare.*

Theodore Roosevelt

*When she inveighed eloquently against
the evils of capitalism . . . she was
conscious of a comfortable feeling that
the system, with all its inequalities and
iniquities, would probably last her time.
It is one of the consolations of
middle-aged reformers that the good they
inculcate must live after them if it is to
live at all.*

Saki (H. H. Munro)

*Nobody talks more of free enterprise
and competition and of the best man
winning than the man who inherited
his father's store or farm.*

C. Wright Mills

*The society of money and exploitation
has never been charged . . . with assuring
the triumph of freedom and justice.*

Albert Camus

*The test of our progress is not whether
we add more to the abundance of those
who have much, it is whether we provide
enough for those who have too little.*

Franklin Delano Roosevelt

*If a free society cannot help the many
who are poor, it cannot save the few
who are rich.*

John F. Kennedy

*Liberty means responsibility. That is why
most men dread it.*

George Bernard Shaw

*When I feed the poor, I am called a saint.
When I ask why the poor are hungry, I
am called a communist.*

Bishop Dom Helder Camara

## THE ONLY THING WE HAVE TO FEAR

It was late in the afternoon in February and getting dark. It was cold. The knock on the front door surprised me because our house is on a busy street with no parking. Visitors park in the alley behind the house and come to our back door. It was far too late in the day for the mail carrier or someone else on a commercial errand. I opened the door to find a gaunt, pale man whose unzipped coat revealed bib overalls and a dark blue shirt. He was bareheaded and bald on top, but the black hair on the sides stuck out away from his head creating a dark halo. He was holding an empty bottle of pills and asking for help.

I tried to understand what it was, exactly, that he wanted from me and as we talked I began to smell the distinct odor of beer on his breath. He was saying something about seizures and the shakiness of his hands suggested that he might have some kind of developmental disability. At one point I heard him say something that sounded like "detox center." I told him to walk to the gas station on the corner and wait for me, that I was going to get my car and drive him to a place where he could get some help.

He was waiting on the corner as I drove up, snow swirling around him from gusts of wind, coat still unzipped. After he got into the car I drove in the direction of the nearest hospital which had a detoxification center. As we approached the hospital the man became agitated and adamantly insisted that he would not go to "any damn hospital." His panic intensified as we came closer to the hospital so I assured him I would not stop. After I drove by the hospital he calmed down. I wondered if he had some kind of mental problem and had been placed in a local apartment as part of the state's deinstitutionalization plan. I have met people who had been confined to an institution for several years and they were usually quite animated in describing their unpleasant experiences in such places. Whether this was his reason for refusing to go to the hospital or not, my problem was what to do with this man. I tried to think of options.

The Salvation Army had a shelter, but I knew they wouldn't accept anyone who was drunk. I couldn't tell if my passenger was drunk or not, but with the alcohol on his breath I assumed he would not be welcome. The only detoxification centers I knew about were at the two hospitals and the city jail. Since it was obvious that a hospital was not acceptable, I considered taking him to the local police station. The man had been talking constantly while I was driving and suddenly he began talking about jail. He had been in jail. He told me how he had been brutalized there. He was beaten and raped and forced to perform oral sex on other prisoners. He begged me not to "call the cops." I couldn't take him to jail.

I was trying to think of other options when he asked that I take him downtown. What began as a request became an insistent demand. Being taken downtown became the only acceptable destination for him. I didn't like it but I didn't know what else to do. I didn't want to take him downtown because of all the bars, but I suspected that he didn't have much money and would not be able to buy a drink. He did not need more alcohol. As we approached Main Street, I drove into a parking lot. I wanted time to think and to suggest some other options. I was hoping I could come up with something better than leaving him downtown.

He did most of the talking. He was eager to talk, but not about his options. He talked about his life, describing several incidents, most of them unpleasant. At one point he noticed a movie marquee visible through the car window behind me and he made a comment about the upcoming movie. I turned to look at the marquee and when I turned back to face him he began apologizing. He assured me that he did not ask me to look away so he could hit me on the head and take my money. That possibility never occurred to me. For the first time I began to be afraid. Why would he say such a thing unless he was considering it? But the man's apology was so sincere that my fear ebbed. Eventually I understood that this action had occurred to him not because he had done it before but probably because it had been done to him.

He asked how old I thought he was. I told him I had never been a good judge of someone's age so I wouldn't even try to guess his, and although I did not guess, he appeared to be close to my age, somewhere around forty. I said he was probably a better judge of age than I was and I asked him to guess my age. He said confidently, "Old enough to be my father." I was so startled by this unexpected comment I just laughed. His tone was apologetic, "I just mean that you are old enough to treat me nice."

We talked a little longer, and then he said he had to go. He offered his hand and I shook it. His palm was moist and sticky. "Do you have any change?" He asked. I gave him what few coins were in my pocket. He shook my hand again. He talked some more. He opened the door, then turned and gave me a kiss on the cheek. He shook my hand and talked some more. One last time he shook my hand and then got out of the car. I watched him walk away until he turned a corner and disappeared. As I drove home, I felt increasingly frustrated by the situation.

When I walked into the house I immediately went to the bathroom to wash my hands, then felt ashamed. I experienced an internal tug-of-war between believing I had done all that I could and feeling I should have done more. I had left the man on the street but his image had not left me, the misery of his existence stuck to me like pine tar. I had scrubbed my hands to erase his touch but I could not erase his words nor his face. It is not easy to remove the stain of someone's suffering once you have been brushed by it.

The previous year I had taught in a special summer program in Austria. Like many other European countries, Austria has a host of human services, including health care, paid for by taxes and available to everyone. They have programs for people with special needs stemming from poverty or a disability or mental illness. These programs are funded primarily by a steeply progressive income tax. Although most Austrians enjoy a comfortable life, only a few can earn enough (or have inherited enough) to live a life of luxury. As one Austrian said, "We have very few really wealthy people here." It is the price they pay to fund their social programs. Like people in other nations, Austrians wonder if they are being too generous in funding programs for their needy and vulnerable people.

It's a legitimate question. In Austria if you lose your job, you can qualify for unemployment compensation based on your previous employment. Their program is similar to what we have in the United States, but it doesn't stop there. The unemployed person can also enroll in one of several job training programs which are government funded. In addition, if a company declares bankruptcy and files proof of inadequate funds to pay their workers, the government will step in and pay the wages owed.

As an incentive to hire disabled workers, the government has passed a law stipulating that for every twenty-five workers a company employs, one worker must be a person with a disability. If the company does not comply it pays a small fine of approximately $155 a month, but it will continue to pay this fine every month until it hires the appropriate number of disabled workers. The money from these fines goes into a fund which is used to reward companies that exceed their quota of disabled workers and this fund also supports projects whose goal is to facilitate the employment of people with a disability. If a company wants to hire a disabled worker but needs to modify its worksite to make it accessible, the company can request money from this fund to make the necessary modifications.

When young men or women graduate from the Austrian equivalent of our high school and cannot find a job, they can enroll in a job training program and apply for government support. This support includes paying rent for an apartment and a small stipend to cover the cost of food and other daily living expenses. If the young person chooses to live at home, he or she would still qualify for a reduced payment toward these living expenses. Government support continues until the young person finds a job.

What would Austria offer the man who came to my door, a man who may have had mental health problems, who might even have been alcoholic and who probably has not been able to find work or keep a job? For the chronically unemployed, including those with chemical dependency problems or mental health problems, the same level of government support is offered. Rent is paid for an apartment and they receive the same stipend for living expenses given to workers who are temporarily unemployed. The only difference is that the monthly stipend will usually be sent to a guardian who is responsible for seeing that the recipient is provided with this money on a daily or weekly basis to ensure that it will be used for living expenses and not to support an addiction. In return for the government's support, individuals must agree to refrain from panhandling. If they violate this rule they could lose all of the benefits being provided by the government.

When I thought of the man I had tried to help and of the limited assistance our society offers him, I was angry. Our lack of compassion is not an accident but a choice made by the voters in our democracy. When pollsters ask U.S. citizens if we should increase assistance to the poor and to those with mental or physical disabilities, the majority usually say the government already does enough. They say anything more should be handled by voluntary efforts or private agencies. When I talk to people about this issue, everyone seems to have a story illustrating an abuse of the welfare system, and the point of each story is to demonstrate the need to cut funding for social service programs. While Austrians wrestle with the real dilemma of determining how much assistance is fair and how much is excessive, Americans wrestle with the question of how much of an illusion of assistance we are willing to fund. From what has happened in recent years, we apparently don't require much of an illusion to satisfy us.

When I have told people about my experience with the man at my door, I am disheartened to hear them commend me for being a good Samaritan, often saying they would have been afraid of the man and probably would not have helped him. People remind me of the mentally ill man in our community who shot and killed a priest and two others in church a few years ago. Although I appreciate their concern, their fear is misplaced. What I learned from my conversation with this unexpected visitor was that he had more to fear from us than we had to fear from him. In his life he had already experienced more brutality and violence than most of us could endure. It is our fear that makes us participants in the oppression of those who suffer. Fear justifies our refusal to fund programs that would offer real compassion and real assistance. Fear prevents us from providing hope to the man at my door and to others who are vulnerable.

We become oppressors because we fail to recognize the humanity of those who suffer. Our unwillingness to hear their painful stories and our willingness to be deceived by the argument that they deserve their misery, as we deserve our comfort, is a major factor in the perpetuation of their pain. Such attitudes destroy any chance for feeling compassion and concern. They take what could make us more human and twist it into something monstrous.

In our culture, far too many of us have become modern versions of medieval torturers—although we may not inflict pain, we allow it to be inflicted. We do not draw and quarter our victims but we draw a deep breath and pitch them a quarter as we pick up our pace and pass them by. We do not handle them with care but we resent them panhandling us. We think we are kind because we smile and say, "Have a nice day." We believe we have enough willpower to ensure that we would never sink so low. We create categories of them and us as exemplars of bad and good. We will not create a more humane, a more caring society until we perceive the absurdity of such distinctions and renounce them. For hundreds of years, wise women and men have proclaimed a simple truth about humanity which we have yet to embrace: there is no "them." We are all part of the human family.

Unfortunately, it is a dysfunctional family. We should not expect miracles. We should not expect to find a world of peace and good will in our lifetimes, but the best hope we have is to challenge people to recognize the common bonds that unite each of us to all other human beings. That perception is essential for the next step: to find fascination and not fear in the differences between people. It is as true today as it was in those dark days when Franklin Roosevelt first told us not to despair, but to trust in each other. The greatest enemy, the only one which has the power to destroy us, is fear. If we are afraid of one another, we will not reach out to help one another, and when we do not reach out to help one another, those who stumble will fall, and some will not get up, and the stench of suffering and death will frighten us even more as we slowly slide down the slippery slope of indifference to our own unremarkable death.

# CHAPTER TWO

## In the Key of B: BENEVOLENCE

### HEAVEN AND HELL
### (A Chinese Tale)

A man once asked God if he could visit heaven and hell. God agreed to take him. When they reached hell the man was amazed to find people seated around a huge banquet table. The finest foods were piled high on this table. What a feast! The smell of the food was so delicious it made the man's mouth water. Perhaps hell was not so bad after all.

But when the man looked closely at the diners, he saw that they were all starving despite the food before them. Each diner had been given chopsticks which were *three feet long!* There was no way the people could carry the food to their mouths with these long chopsticks. No one could eat a bite. What a hell indeed, to sit so close to a banquet and yet be unable to taste a morsel. The man wept because their suffering was so terrible.

The man was then taken to heaven to observe life there. To his surprise he saw people seated around a banquet table in exactly the same situation. The finest foods were piled high on the table and each person had been given three-foot long chopsticks. As it was in hell, so it was in heaven! But here everyone was well fed and happy. The man looked around and marveled at all the people laughing and talking. He turned to God and asked how this could be. "It is simple but it requires a certain skill," said God. The man was still confused, "What skill do you mean?"

"It is not difficult. You see, they have learned to feed each other" [1, p. 72].

Although altruism is important, it is not sufficient by itself to ensure positive human relations. The experience of the Kwakiutl described in the previous chapter illustrates this problem. The U.S. government could have claimed that it was merely acting on its concern for the well-being of the Kwakiutl people, but its concern for individual progress

29

was destructive to the harmony of the group. By imposing its cultural values on the Kwakiutl, the U.S. government may have believed its actions were for their benefit, but to the Kwakiutl it must have felt like being chastised by an authoritarian parent. There was concern, but no kindness in this action.

> **Benevolence**—desiring to do good . . . characterized by good will (kindhearted) . . . organized for the purpose of doing good . . . intended for benefits rather than profit.

When people are perceived as altruistic it is assumed that they are kind, and a person described as benevolent is assumed to be altruistic as well. Yet there are people who engage in altruistic behavior not from a desire to be kind but from a sense of duty or a commitment to a cause. Certain crusaders for Christ have come to college campuses to warn students against participating in various behaviors considered sinful. In their desire to save each student's soul, some of the evangelists have stalked the campuses, loudly accosting students as they are walking to class and commanding them to repent of their sins. The motivation of these evangelists may stem from an altruistic concern for the students, but their intimidating, belligerent behavior suggests that benevolence has little to do with it.

Benevolence is about doing good, about being kind. Too often it is defined by a singular act. Someone saves a child from drowning and that one act creates a perception of that individual as a good person. Later if the same person is caught committing a crime or engaged in some other misbehavior people shake their heads and wonder how such a good person could do that. I suspect that many of those who seem oblivious to the needs of people they see everyday would respond appropriately if given an opportunity to do a good deed which was likely to garner attention and praise. In a media age, everyone is looking for their fifteen minutes of fame. Such an opportunity may never come, but meanwhile they will have wasted countless opportunities to engage in simple acts of kindness.

If a person believes in a particular value, we would expect that person not only to engage in behavior reflecting that value but also to encourage such behavior in others. A benevolent person should be willing to accept help from another if help is offered, but there are people who often help others yet do not accept help in return. If questioned, they would usually say they did not want to feel obligated to others. They want to be free to decide whom they will help and when they will help. Is it benevolent to be kind to some people but ignore the misery of others? What does it mean if a person only engages in benevolent activities some of the time and only with certain people? Can we call a person benevolent who is willing to help a friend but does not respond to the plea of a stranger? One would not have to value benevolence to engage in random acts of kindness, but valuing benevolence seems necessary to being a kind person. Valuing benevolence should result in unconditional kindness.

Those who will only help certain people at certain times presumably view themselves as good human beings. Their efforts to help others are probably motivated by a desire to act in a manner consistent with this view. Helping others affirms a positive perception of themselves, whereas receiving help from others does not. Even though other people would probably perceive them and even describe them as benevolent, the reluctance of such people to accept help suggests that their behavior may be as self-serving as it is charitable.

> **Independence**—not influenced, guided or controlled by others, not relying on others for aid or support . . . refusing to accept help from or be under obligation to others . . . possessing sufficient financial resources to be free of another's control or of the need to work.

The reason some charitable people don't want to receive charity is because they cherish their independence. Being independent means being able to take care of one's own needs. To be independent is to refuse to accept help from others because that creates an obligation to return the favor. Anything that detracts from making decisions unaffected by outside influences is considered a liability. People who value independence will remain as free of entanglements as possible. People who value independence may refuse to accept someone's help, especially financial assistance, while striving to achieve the ultimate goal of independence: to have so much money that the person no longer needs to work to live comfortably.

If independence is desired, it can curb the desire to be benevolent. The benevolent person profits from the pleasure of helping others and not from any tangible compensation. To the person who gives a high priority to being independent, benevolent behavior is a waste of time. If the end one desires is independence, then money is the means to that end and time is money. Valuing independence is the foundation for the concept of the self-made man who believes he is solely responsible for his success. The ultimate goal of the self-made man is to achieve freedom which is defined as being free from any financial or personal obligations to others.

The way to achieve such freedom is to succeed without help from others. It can't be achieved if one is distracted by the problems of others or involved in helping them solve their problems. In the Chinese tale about Heaven and Hell, what sort of response should be expected from the person who values independence? Such a person would surely remain hungry rather than accept a morsel of food offered by another, but the benevolent person would gratefully accept the food and offer a bite of food in return. Kindness is a gift, and whether one gives or receives it, it is a gift which is valued by any person who places a high priority on benevolence.

## ❧ ❧ ❧
## *HEARING VOICES*

*The fool hath said in his heart: There is no God. . . . there is none that doeth good, no not one.*

Book of Common Prayer

*Of all the preposterous assumptions of humanity over humanity, nothing exceeds most of the criticisms made on the habits of the poor by the well-housed, well-warmed, well-fed.*

Herman Melville

*I expect to pass through this world but once. If therefore, there be any kindness I can show, or any good thing I can do to any fellow being, let me do it now, and not defer or neglect it, as I shall not pass this way again.*

William Penn

*On reflecting at dinner that he had done nothing to help anybody all day, the Emperor Titus remarked "Friends, I have lost a day."*

Suetonius

*A man makes no noise over a good
deed, but passes on to another.*
                    Marcus Aurelius

*Seek not goodness from without, seek it
within yourselves, or you will never
find it.*
                              Epictetus

*Real joy comes not from riches or
from the praise of man, but from
doing something worthwhile.*
                    Sir Wilfred Grenfell

*If a rich man is proud of his wealth, he
should not be praised until it is known
how he employs it.*
                              Socrates

*The only thing necessary for the triumph
of evil is for good men to do nothing.*
                    Edmund Burke

*Goodness is the only investment that
never fails.*
                    Henry David Thoreau

*So many gods, so many creeds,
So many paths that wind and wind,
While just the art of being kind
Is all the sad world needs.*
                    Emma Wheeler Wilcox

*We do not quite forgive a giver. The hand
that feeds us is in some danger of being
bitten.*
                    Ralph Waldo Emerson

*Part of kindness is loving people more than they deserve.*

Joseph Jourbert

*You can accomplish anything by kindness, what you cannot do by force.*

Publius Syrus

*Kindness in words creates confidence. Kindness in thinking creates profound- ness. Kindness in giving creates love.*

Lao Tzu

*I am only one, but still I am one. I cannot do everything, but still I can do something. I will not refuse to do the something I can do.*

Helen Keller

*Criticism is something we can avoid easily—by saying nothing, doing nothing, being nothing.*

Aristotle

*A good person takes as much trouble to discover what is right as lesser people take to discover what will pay.*

Confucius

*It takes a very clever person to turn cynic and a wise person to be clever enough not to.*

Fannie Hurst

*Here lies one who meant well, tried a little, failed much: — surely that may be his epitaph, of which he need not be ashamed.*

Robert Louis Stevenson

## A SMALL VICTORY

*Be ashamed to die until you have won
some victory for humanity.*
Horace Mann

Uncle Vernie died. He was eighty-one. It was not unexpected. He had been on dialysis, had lost the use of his legs, had been overweight for most of his life, and he had gone to the hospital for a hernia operation. Despite the risks, the doctors thought his chances of survival were good, but he didn't survive.

The death of a family member or a friend often serves to remind us of our own mortality and prompts us to reflect on our lives. The long drive to attend my Uncle's funeral provided an opportunity for such reflection. First came the facts of my Uncle's life. He was a veteran of World War II including the Battle of the Bulge and Remagen Bridge. Returning to his Nebraska home, he worked at various jobs until he became the janitor at the high school. Vernie never married. After retirement he lived in his hometown until health problems forced him into the Veterans Home in Grand Island. His health problems were a result of smoking three packs of cigarettes a day until he was hospitalized with emphysema and ordered to quit smoking. He had lived in the Veterans Home for the last ten years. He was a large but gentle man. I had always liked Uncle Vernie.

The funeral home on Main Street was next to Thomsen's Corner, a bar where Vernie had enjoyed a beer or two . . . or more. Across the street was the restaurant where Vernie ate his midnight meals of steak, potatoes, and beer after coming home from driving a truck for several hours across several states. This had been familiar terrain to Uncle Vernie, but it was not familiar to me, only dimly accessible in fading childhood memories.

The funeral was conducted by my cousin, a Presbyterian minister. His comments in the eulogy corresponded to my reflections on the road. Uncle Vernie had been a kind man, a good neighbor, a reliable friend. Not simply an exercise in "speaking well of the dead," this was an accurate description of Vernie's life, yet it would have embarrassed him if he had heard his nephew standing up there saying all of these things in front of everyone. Even before the funeral started I had been reminded of Vernie's kindness when a woman unknown to me approached the coffin using a walker to support her. She appeared to be in her mid-thirties. She stared at Vernie for a long time. As she turned to walk away, tears were flowing down her cheeks. I whispered to my cousin, "Who is she?" I was told that she had been born with her disability and later her mother and father separated. Even before the parents got a divorce

Vernie began to drive the little girl to school and to music lessons after school. He was her personal chauffeur. I had not been aware of this, and Vernie, of course, never mentioned it.

For my cousin and his siblings, Vernie had played an especially important role. He was not just their kind and generous Uncle but an ally when dealing with their alcoholic and abusive father. After their mother died, the four children she left behind turned to Uncle Vernie and Grandma Koppelman for support and stability, and the two of them became surrogate parents. When Grandma died, Vernie was left to play the role alone. Uncle Vernie was always there to care for them and later for their children after they married and started their own families.

Vernie quit his truck driving job to become the janitor at the high school. In addition to his normal duties, teachers often asked him to make something the school could not afford to buy—something for the set of the Junior Class Play, or for the display at the banquet for the Senior Prom, or something the coaches needed for the track team. He always managed to give them what they wanted. He once said, "I am not just a custodian of a school building; I am also the custodian of the kids." That's probably why he cut plywood into Santa shapes and painted Santa on them and donated them as decorations for Main Street at Christmas. He made a similar Santa for his brother's children, except our plywood Santa was posed in front of a painted fireplace with three small stockings, one for each of us children. It became a family tradition. Every Christmas in front of our house there was Santa pointing to the stockings on the fireplace mantle. Although battered by winter weather, it has survived the ravages of time. Every Christmas when I visit my older sister it is there to greet me on her front lawn.

What I have said so far is merely the tip of the iceberg. Uncle Vernie did things for people, all the time. He was not the sort of man to say he was too busy or too tired or didn't want to. If you asked him for help, you got it, usually right away, and frequently you got his help without asking for it. I have often wondered, and I wondered again on the way to his funeral, "Why did Uncle Vernie do this?"

Vernie was not a religious man; he seemed allergic to the air inside a church. One of the stories my cousin told in the eulogy was of a time when Vernie entered a local restaurant and saw the three Protestant ministers at one table talking and drinking coffee. They called him over to gently chide him about not going to church. During this conversation one of them said, "Vernie, how are you going to explain this when you meet your maker?" Vernie said, "I'll tell him he sent three of the best and they all failed." He laughed. And they laughed with him.

If religion doesn't explain his willingness to help others, what does? I recently talked to a colleague who deplored the lack of commitment to community and service among the current crop of professors. He claimed they were self-serving professionals whose every decision was based on career considerations, and that the few exceptions to this rule were almost always those whose background included military service. I have never served in the military but I remember my brother-in-law's descriptions of marine training that stripped away your individuality to make you think and act in terms of your squad. Was Vernie's army experience in World War II the basis for his benevolence?

I had difficulty accepting this explanation. My cousins' alcoholic and abusive father was also a veteran, and he was not kind. In addition, Vernie's opinions often differed from those of other veterans. This was one of the reasons I always enjoyed talking to him. The commemoration of VJ day during the summer of 1995 had renewed the controversy over whether or not we should have dropped the atomic bomb on Hiroshima and Nagasaki. Letters to the editor in the local paper from many veterans expressed support for the decision because it saved American lives. When I raised the issue with Vernie, he said the bomb didn't have to be used, that Japan was ready to surrender. He deplored the loss of life and the destruction caused by this action.

My father did not serve in the military, but he is a kind and generous man. He has a history of helping neighbors, serving on school boards and town boards, and doing other thankless tasks that were necessary for the good of his community. This was also true of my Aunt Elaine, a nurse who was genuinely beloved in her community. She was known to give away sample pills to people who had been prescribed medications they couldn't afford. She made house calls to give shots to sick children and stayed to care for them if they were seriously ill. She volunteered at her church and in her community, and when she died unexpectedly during minor surgery at the age of forty-two almost everyone in the community came to her funeral. I will never forget the weeping and groaning of these normally stoic people as they filed past her coffin. It occurred to me that this concern for others was perhaps simply part of the values my grandparents taught and modeled for their children.

The more I considered this, the less persuaded I became. My grandparents were the children of immigrants; both came from Germany but my grandmother's parents came from Schleswig, which is near the border of Germany and Denmark. Both families had farms in northeastern Nebraska where Bill and Mary met through a mutual friend. Bill left his father's farm to work on the railroad, and eventually he opened a blacksmith shop. He worked hard, drank hard and shared his money freely with his friends, especially when he was buying drinks at the bar. My grandparents had fierce and frequent arguments about money, based largely on Bill's inability to manage it, but he stubbornly insisted that controlling the money was a man's responsibility. He eventually lost the argument and my grandmother was able to save some money for their retirement years which were few for him, one of the consequences of his hard life.

On the other hand, whenever people talked about my grandparents, they usually did not refer to their poverty but to their generosity. They remember how patient Bill was with the farmers who were slow to pay their bills. He would never ask them to pay for the handful of nails they would stuff into their pockets on the way out of the blacksmith shop. Mary's generosity was usually a spontaneous gesture. Once my mother was visiting her mother-in-law and drinking coffee when she mentioned how pretty the sugar bowl was. Mary immediately got up and took the sugar bowl into the kitchen, dumped the contents into another bowl, rinsed and wiped it out, and handed it to my mother as a gift. My mother tried to refuse, but Mary insisted. Many of my grandmother's friends, especially the women who played cards with her, told similar stories about her. Possessions did not mean much to my grandmother; people did.

Although my grandparents were not perfect parents, their spirit of generosity, of helping others, of sharing what little they had might explain, at least in part, Uncle Vernie's kindness to others. My wife remembers her grandparents also being generous toward others. She believes this was characteristic of the generation that lived through the Great Depression. Her grandfather worked for the railroad during the hard times and because of his job he had to have a phone at home. Neighbors would come over to use the phone, and if her grandmother happened to be baking bread the visitor would usually leave with a loaf.

Did the hard times of the 1930s mold a generation of Americans into being concerned for the welfare of others and committed to helping them? On the surface this seems a plausible explanation, yet authors like John Steinbeck have written eloquently of the cruelty inflicted on the most vulnerable people during this time. When my father was hitchhiking out to California in search of a job, hunger forced him to knock on doors, asking for work or food or both. Many doors were slammed in his face. He was more likely to receive something at the more humble homes. He remembers knocking on the door of a rundown shack and being told brusquely to wait. In a few minutes the door opened and a sandwich was thrust toward him. It was a gift my father appreciated whether graciously or grudgingly given.

Many people have had similar experiences and yet these affect different people in different ways. There may be no simple answer for why some develop a generous spirit and others do not, but hard times like the Great Depression remind us of our human frailty and of our common destiny. In response to a question about long-term economic consequences, John Maynard Keynes said, "In the long run, we are all dead." Perhaps this is the answer; perhaps a consciousness of one's mortality is necessary before one can have compassion for others.

Several factors may contribute to the creation of a generous spirit. Military comradeship, role models, even the brutality of poverty can teach us about common human needs. In addition, various religions encourage compassion and a commitment to ease the suffering of others, but some people question whether contemporary institutionalized religions still teach such lessons. Returning from a study trip to Israel, my daughter Tess sat next to a woman who described her journey as a pilgrimage and identified herself as a Baptist. Asked about her faith, Tess said she didn't believe in any particular religion. When she saw the woman's smile fading Tess added that she believed in helping people and trying to make the world a better place. The woman's face simply grew longer, but she assured Tess that there was still time to find Jesus, still time to save her soul.

I'm sure the woman's concern for Tess's soul reflected her deep convictions, but blithely ignoring Tess's commitment to helping others raises questions about what lessons this woman had learned from reading the Bible. There are many interpretations, but one obvious commitment for a Christian is to respond to human needs and human suffering. Christians are challenged to serve others not only when it is convenient but whenever the need arises. Such help is to be given regardless of whether the person needing help is a Christian or not, heterosexual or not, freely given whether or not that person is deserving of help. After one recent and thoughtful discussion, a friend of mine who is a minister explained it this way:

> Since the belief in the undeserved salvation of one's soul and the gratitude that this engenders is what frees and compels a Christian to practice Christ-like compassion for "the least of these," Christians should be energetically involved in efforts to respond to the human needs of others for the sake of the other, confidently (and in faith) leaving the care of their souls to God [2].

As our society becomes increasingly diverse and as we become part of the global village, we need to renew our understanding of the responsibility we owe to each other and offer a helping hand, remembering our common destiny and affirming our common needs. Some might dismiss this proposal as impractical, but Uncle Vernie left a legacy of good works to prove that it is possible to do good without being a saint. Just as I can imagine Vernie's embarrassment at his eulogy, I can also imagine Uncle Vernie laughing at any attempt to link him in any way to saintly behavior. All Vernie did was simply to say yes when he was asked to help, and sometimes to offer help without being asked.

Too often benevolent acts are limited to giving away outgrown clothes or toys the children don't play with or other token contributions. In order to reinforce the value of being kind to others, helping others, some high schools have introduced a graduation requirement mandating that each student complete a minimum number of hours on community service activities. To some degree these requirements are based on the success of volunteer programs for youth which have emerged in recent years, programs like City Year.

During a trip to Boston I visited the City Year program. This program provided the city's disadvantaged youth with opportunities to help others in the community. As a reward the young people earned a high school diploma if they didn't already have one, and they were guaranteed admission into a technical school or college in Boston at the end of the year. They also received a small salary. Part of the routine for visitors was to eat lunch with some program participants. During lunch on the day I was there, one visitor asked, "What do you get out of this?" A blonde, rugged looking eighteen year old sitting next to me looked at the questioner thoughtfully, then he said, "I think a lot of us come into the program thinking like that, thinking about the money they pay you now and the money they promise you later, but about halfway through the year you realize that you are getting more from the program just by what you are doing to help people." He said it simply and sincerely. Uncle Vernie would have understood.

A rabbi in Kansas City told me about a book which described the people who helped Jews escape or hid them during the Holocaust. He said they were a diverse group of people with little in common except they had all had some experience during their childhood which made them unable to accept the Nazi denunciation of the Jews. Some had played with Jews as children; some had parents who taught them that all people are part of God's creation and who treated all people with dignity and respect. His comment made me wonder if perhaps ethical behavior is a result of what could be called *ethical memories*. Words may provide guidance, but words without deeds are stillborn. The moral influence of parents or others who say one thing and do another is minimal at best, but our experiences with people who consistently act with kindness and generosity toward others can have a profound impact. If this is true, we must find ways to provide such experiences for our children and youth because life offers only a haphazard curriculum. Schools and community agencies and programs like City Year need to make sure children and youth have experiences which can create such ethical memories.

Horace Mann said, "Be ashamed to die until you have won some victory for humanity." Uncle Vernie helped others when it wasn't convenient, volunteered his time when he had other things to do, shared his money when there wasn't much to share. He did this willingly, without asking for anything in return. This was his achievement, and it was more important than his participation in the battles of World War II. Uncle Vernie achieved a victory for humanity. Some might say it was a small one and Vernie would probably agree, but even a small victory is a good one. Vernie had no reason to feel ashamed. Rest in peace.

## ECHOES

*The man who makes no mistakes does not usually make anything.*

        Edward John Phelps

*It is not the critic who counts, not the one who points out . . . where the doer of good deeds could have done better. The credit belongs to the one who is actually in the arena; whose face is marred by dust and sweat and blood, who strives valiantly, who errs and comes short again and again . . . his place shall never be with those cold and timid souls who know neither victory nor defeat.*

        Theodore Roosevelt

*Generous people are rarely mentally ill people.*

        Karl Menninger

*The question should never be who is right, but what is right.*

        Glenn Gardiner

*The only person with whom you
should try to get even, are those who
have helped you.*

May Maloo

*The best index to a person's character is
how he treats people who can't do him
any good, and how he treats people who
can't fight back.*

Abigail Van Buren

*Capital as such is not evil, it is its
wrong use that is evil.*

Mohandis K. Gandhi

*The sad truth is that most evil is done
by people who never make up their
minds to be either good or evil.*

Hannah Arendt

*The trouble with the rat race is that
even if you win, you're still a rat.*

Lily Tomlin

*The future is not designed by the great
events, but by the small things that
people do wherever they are.*

Poshimi Mayuar

*Democracy is measured not by its leaders
doing extraordinary things, but by its
citizens doing things extraordinarily
well.*

John Gardner

*No man can be good for long if goodness
is not in demand.*

Bertolt Brecht

*You need more tact in the dangerous
art of giving than in any other social
action.*

William Bolitho

*Love that is not expressed in loving
actions does not really exist, just as
talent that does not express itself in
creative works does not exist; neither
of these is a state of mind, or feeling,
but an activity . . . or a myth.*

Sidney Harris

*Do not wait for leaders; do it alone,
person to person.*

Mother Teresa

*The vast majority of Americans, who are
comparatively well off, have developed
an ability to have enclaves of people
living in the greatest misery without
almost noticing them.*

Gunnar Myrdal

*It's not what you do once in awhile,
It's what you do day in and day out
That makes the difference.*

Jenny Craig

*Do not follow where the path may lead.
Go instead where there is no path and
leave a trail.*

Muriel Strode

*The human race advances only by the
extra achievements of the individual.
You are the individual.*

Charles Towne

## BUCKY BOGGS WOULD NEVER DIE

I remember the gunfights. Standing behind a tree or crouched behind a bush or peering around the corner of the house, gun cocked and ready, looking for the enemy. We only used caps in the guns in late June when they were purchased along with the Fourth of July fireworks, and we used them sparingly so they would last as long as possible. Most of the time we used our voices for the sound effects since the tiny "click" of the toy gun was not adequate for serious gunfighting. We knew what a real gunfight should sound like—we had been to the movies! So we cocked our guns and pulled the trigger shouting "Bang!" in a voice loud enough to mask that pathetic "click."

All my friends liked to play this game. We would spend long summer afternoons running for cover, shooting and shouting and clutching an arm in mock pain as an imaginary bullet wounded us. The game ended when someone decided to die. This usually involved a lot of staggering and moaning and perhaps even a spin or two before collapsing in a heap on the ground. There were no formal rules to this game, but it was an unspoken agreement that the players would take turns being the one to die. There was only one problem. Bucky Boggs would never die.

When he began coming to my house to play, I didn't realize Bucky had this idiosyncrasy. I appreciated the dramatic possibilities of dying and that made it easy for me to take my turn as the one who was shot and killed. I created ever more elaborate death agonies and enjoyed the challenge of coming up with new improvisations, but as much as I liked it, nobody wants to die all the time. It becomes tedious, and it just wasn't fair. After I realized that Bucky would not take his turn at being killed, I devised a strategy to force him to die.

It was obvious that I had to get closer to him. I tried to claim mortal shots from a distance, but Bucky would just laugh and shout "You missed me!" I had to shoot him at such close range he could not claim that I had missed. The next time he came to play, I got my gun and we took our positions behind two trees. After exchanging a few shots, I dashed for the tree he was hiding behind. When he looked around the tree and saw me coming he fired at me and I grabbed my right shoulder with my free left hand as if in pain but still pointed my gun right at Bucky and fired. I couldn't have been more than ten feet away. He grabbed his right shoulder even though I had aimed at his head and then he shot again aiming at my head. By now he had me at point blank range. There was nothing for me to do but die, once again.

I got up off the ground and we started over. This time I took my position behind the corner of my house. We each fired a shot and then I crept away and quietly opened the back door so Bucky would not hear what I was doing. I ran through the house and opened the front door quietly and started sneaking up behind him. The plan was working. Bucky was peering around the tree, gun pointed at the corner of the house, waiting for me to stick my head out. He did not hear me as I crept up carefully behind him. When I was about three feet away, I pointed my gun at the back of his head, pulled the trigger and shouted "Bang!" Bucky was so startled at the sound of my voice he spun around and stumbled backward. Instead of falling down dead, he fired his gun at me. I could not believe it, "Hey, you can't shoot me! You're dead!" He looked right at me with a wicked smile and touched the back of his head, "Oh, that? It was just a flesh wound." That's when I knew that it would not matter what I did, Bucky Boggs would never die. It bothered me so much that I only played with Bucky if there was no one else around.

This past summer I was driving through a residential area when I heard a child's voice shout "Bang!" and I saw a boy fall backward to the ground. I smiled as memories of childhood came back to me, and for the first time in a long time I remembered Bucky Boggs. As I recalled our gunfights, I wondered why he would not die. I tried to remember his family. Although no one was wealthy in the village where I grew up, Bucky's family was worse off than most. There were five children, two boys and three girls and a mother who did not not have the energy nor the temperament needed to raise five children, especially when their father would spend as much time sitting on a bar stool drinking beer as he did at work. The discipline strategy for both parents was to slap their children on the head anytime they did something wrong. These were not gentle slaps. I flinched more than once as I watched Bucky absorb these blows. He never cried. I respected his toughness.

Bucky was only a year younger and he lived one block from my house so we played together since we were toddlers. When we got older we played competitive sports, especially basketball and baseball. Bucky could not beat me in any kind of athletic competition, and he was even less of a threat when it came to competing for good grades in school.

We went to a one-room country school with children from kindergarten through the eighth grade. Near the end of my sixth grade year, the teacher surprised everyone by announcing that every child would be promoted except for one. She thought Bucky should repeat the fifth grade again next year. This would have put Bucky in the same grade as his younger brother. The cruelty and humiliation of this stunning announcement overwhelmed him. It was the only time I ever saw Bucky cry. I felt sorry for him. Ultimately the teacher promoted him, and Bucky seemed to be more careful about handing in his homework on time and being prepared for tests. Perhaps that was the purpose of her announcement, to scare Bucky into being more diligent and conscientious about his school work. If so, it was a cruel but effective strategy.

These memories reminded me how much more difficult life had been for Bucky. He had not been blessed with good parents, nor had he been given any special talent as compensation. There was one victory he could achieve by sheer determination: he could win the gunfights. That's probably why Bucky refused to die. He needed to be successful at something, and this game was his best chance. No matter what happened, Bucky would be the one standing over the prone body of his defeated opponent. What he could not have in reality, he would have in this fantasy.

Human beings have needs, and if we're fortunate many of them will be satisfied by family or friends or neighbors, or sometimes through the kindness of strangers. We have all heard reference to the "truly needy" or "deserving poor" to distinguish between those we want to help and those we do not. People don't mind helping the unemployed man who was laid off and can't find a job even though he's looking everywhere for work, but we don't want to help the man who seems shiftless as he drifts from job to job and wastes what little money he gets on cigarettes and beer. We don't mind helping the welfare mother with two children who was abandoned by her husband, but we don't want to help the welfare mother who had two children by two different fathers and was not married to either. Their needs are the same, but Americans today seem reluctant to provide assistance to the "undeserving" poor [3].

As a freshman in high school, two of my friends were boys from families with serious financial problems. I went to Frank's home once and it was obvious that the family had too many children and not enough money. The family scraped by from paycheck to paycheck. Rick's situation was even worse. He lived with his mother. No one knew where his father was. There were rumors that his mother was on welfare, that she was mentally ill. I was never invited to his home. Whenever I would ask Frank or Rick to go to the movies or something else that cost money, they would say they had other things to do. I always wondered if they just didn't have the money. We never talked about it.

One day after track practice in early spring, the three of us walked downtown to the corner cafe to get Cokes. As we drank and talked, we drifted into the bowling alley connected to the cafe. The bowling alley was open all day on weekends, but during the week it was only open in the evenings. The bowling lanes were dark. The only light came through the plate glass window next to the street entrance, and it was getting dark outside.

We walked over by the cash register which had a large Easter Seals canister sitting next to it. I leaned my arm on top of the right side of the cash register and my friends stood on the other side. Frank stared at the canister and wondered aloud how much money it contained. I picked it up and said it felt heavy so it must be almost full. They talked about taking it, but I assumed it was just talk. Finally Rick said to me, "Push the can over here and I'll slip it into my coat." It sounded like a dare, so after looking at the entryway leading into the cafe and seeing no one, I pushed the canister to the other side of the cash register. I was stunned when Rick stuck the canister in his coat and started walking toward the door. Frank walked out behind him. After a moment's hesitation, I hurried after them.

After walking a couple of blocks we entered an alley and crouched behind a fence where we couldn't be seen. Rick broke open the canister and he and Frank counted the money. Although it was mostly nickels and dimes, there might have been as much as $12 in change. My friends wanted to divide it equally among us, but I said I didn't want any. I had a sick, scared feeling in the pit of my stomach and I wanted nothing to do with that money. They didn't mind giving me a smaller share, but they insisted that I take something, perhaps less from a desire to share the wealth than from a desire to share the guilt. Whatever the reason, they demanded that I tell them how much I wanted. I told them to give me a dollar's worth of dimes which they did. As they were dividing the rest of the coins between them, I told them I had to go. I walked for a few minutes before I began throwing the dimes away, one at a time, every last one of them, but it was easier to rid myself of the coins than the guilt I felt from the theft of that money.

The outcome of this crime surprised me as much as the crime itself. A few days later I heard someone joking about Frank and Rick paying their class dues. The dues were four dollars a year and anyone who didn't pay at any time during our four years in high school would not be allowed to participate in Senior Sneak Day where all the seniors skipped school for a day and boarded a bus bound for some exotic place like Omaha. This trip was always scheduled shortly before the end of the senior year. Frank and Rick had not paid their dues and the school year was almost over. At the beginning of the study period they dumped eight dollars in coins, mostly nickels and dimes, on the desk of the class treasurer, much to his surprise and much to the annoyance of the teacher supervising the study area. Frank and Rick acted as if it was just a joke, but I was the only one who saw the embarrassment behind the bravado. I knew where the money came from.

The fact that my friends would use money stolen from charity to pay their class dues made a powerful impression on me. It was the first time I really understood just how poor they were. The families of my other friends were financially secure, so paying four dollars for class dues was not a dilemma for them. Knowing that Frank and Rick used the money for this purpose made me feel a little less guilty about the theft. It wasn't right for them to steal, but for them, as for most teenagers, the need to belong is paramount. They did what they had to do.

Although the need to belong is powerful, their willingness to steal surely cast my friends into the realm of the undeserving poor, at least for those who use such terms. Although the attitudes reflected by such language may seem to be a recent development, they are not new. In George Bernard Shaw's *Pygmalion,* Mr. Doolittle provides his analysis:

> I'm one of the undeserving poor: that's what I am. Think of what that means to a man. It means that he's up agen middle class morality all the time. If there's anything going, and I put in for a bit of it, it's always the same story: "You're undeserving; so you can't have it." But my needs is as great as the most deserving widow's that ever got money out of six different charities in one week for the death of the same husband. I don't need less than a deserving man: I need more. I don't eat less hearty than him; and I drink a lot more. I want a bit of amusement, cause I'm a thinking man. I want cheerfulness and a song and a band when I feel low. Well, they charge me just the same for everything as they charge the deserving. What is middle class morality? Just an excuse for never giving me anything [4, p. 58].

Henry Higgins proclaims Mr. Doolittle a philosopher. Although Higgins might agree that Doolittle should do more to meet his own needs, it is true that his needs are the same as other poor people, regardless of why he can't meet them. To refuse help to someone because he or she is perceived as undeserving calls into question our ideas about benevolence. Benevolence is an act of kindness toward another. Should kindness be withheld because the recipient is deemed unworthy? Is this the act of a benevolent person? Benevolence is not merely the act of offering assistance, but offering assistance without conditions, an act of random kindness.

Because I have been the recipient of benevolence, I have learned to appreciate its value. My wife and I married in the middle of our senior year in college and moved into a duplex. I had one semester of classes to complete while my wife was working with high school seniors as a student teacher. One warm spring afternoon the supervising teacher suggested that the students gather outside to talk about their poetry assignment. While they sat on the grass discussing tropes and misanthropes, someone saw my wife's purse under the teacher's desk in the deserted classroom and took the $50 she happened to have that day so she could stop at the supermarket on her way home from school. For a young couple with college tuition in addition to household bills and only a part-time job to pay for them, this loss was a catastrophe.

The next day an elderly woman with white hair came to the door collecting for cancer. I was still depressed by the theft. I apologized for not giving her anything, but I explained about the money being stolen. She was sorry and told me not to worry and then she left. A few minutes later she was back knocking at the door. She told me she lived across the street and pointed out her home. She invited me to come over and talk to her if I thought of anything she could do. Although I couldn't imagine how she could help, I appreciated her offer.

About thirty minutes later there was another knock on the door. It was the white haired woman again with an envelope in her hand. She was talking fast and seemed embarrassed, but she was saying something about how easy it was to give to charity and forget about the people nearby who could use some help. She handed me the envelope and told me she wanted me to take it. She was so insistent and I was so surprised that I took it without comment. She said I didn't need to say anything but she hoped it would help and then she left. Inside the envelope was a ten dollar bill. She had not waited for me to thank her.

Her name was Mrs. McKinney. She was a widow living on Social Security in the two-story white frame house she had pointed out to me. Later I would have more conversations with her and we became better acquainted, but when she handed me that envelope she knew nothing except my financial need. She didn't ask what political party I belonged to or what church I attended or even if I attended church at all. She didn't ask for my views on the Vietnam war or abortion. She didn't ask me if I drank alcohol or smoked cigarettes or used drugs. She simply responded to my need with her gift. That day, Mrs. McKinney became my model for benevolence.

When my wife came home, I told her what happened and she was touched by Mrs. McKinney's kindness. I tried to return the money, but Mrs. McKinney refused to take it. She suggested that I could mow her lawn sometime. Later that spring I did mow her lawn, and afterwards she called my wife to invite us to her house for supper. In July my wife gave birth to our first child, and we invited Mrs. McKinney to our house to see him. I still have the photograph of Mrs. McKiney holding our baby boy on her lap.

After graduation my wife and I were offered teaching jobs and we moved away. We exchanged Christmas cards with Mrs. McKinney for a few years until the year one of her children wrote to say she had passed away. Mrs. McKiney was gone, but her memory lives on. In the midst of dark thoughts that threaten to cast all humanity into the mire of selfishness, Mrs. McKinney reminds me that kindness also has a place in the human heart. Her kindness expressed in deeds what Albert Schweitzer expressed in these words:

> I look back upon my youth and realize how so many people gave me help, understanding, courage . . . They entered into my life and became powers within me. All of us live spiritually by what others have given us, often unwittingly . . .We all owe to others much of gentleness and wisdom that we have made our own, and we may well ask ourselves what will others owe us [5, p. 67].

To be the recipient of kindness is to be told that you are worthy of such kindness, and that alone is the value of benevolence. Knowing that a stranger believed I was worth helping meant more to me than the money she gave me. Mrs. McKinney was a person with a benevolent spirit, and whenever I help someone, I am remembering her and honoring her memory. It is also an illustration of this meditation on ten strong things which appears in the Talmud:

> There are ten strong things. Iron is strong, but fire melts it. Fire is strong, but water quenches it. Water is strong, but the sun evaporates it. The sun is strong, but clouds cover it. Clouds are strong, but winds can drive the clouds away. Wind is strong, but man can shut it out. Man is strong, but fears cast him down. Fear is strong, but sleep overcomes it. Sleep is strong, yet death is stronger. But the strongest is kindness. It survives death.

# CHAPTER THREE
## In the Key of C:  COLLABORATION

### THE PURPOSE OF EDUCATION

Years ago in England when the workingmen, starving in the mines and factories, gathered in mobs and took bread wherever they could get it, their friends tried to educate them into a knowledge of the causes of their poverty and degradation. At one of these "monster bread meetings," held in Manchester, John Bright said to them, "Workingmen, what you need to bring to you cheap bread and plenty of it, is the franchise"; but they shouted back to Mr. Bright, "It is not the vote we want, it is bread." But at length, through the persistent demands of a handful of reformers, there was introduced into the British Parliament the "household suffrage" bill of 1867 . . . the opposition was championed by Robert Lowe, who presented all the stock objections to the extension of the franchise . . . the same that would be later used against giving the vote to women . . . But the bill became law; and before the session closed, it was Robert Lowe who moved that Parliament, having enfranchised these men, should now make an appropriation for the establishment and support of schools for the education of them and their sons saying, "Unless they are educated . . . they will be the means of overturning the throne of England."

So long as the poor men in the mines and factories had not the right to vote, the power to make and unmake laws and lawmakers, to help or hurt the government, no measure ever had been proposed for their benefit although they were ground under the heel of the capitalist to a condition of abject slavery. But the moment this power was placed in their hands, before they have used it even once, the bitterest enemy to their possessing it is the first man to spring to his feet and make this motion for the most beneficent measure possible in their behalf—public schools for the education of themselves and their children [1, pp. 138-139].

> **Collaboration**—laboring together to produce a product . . . working together for a common purpose . . . acting jointly to achieve a common goal . . . cooperation with an enemy given by an inhabitant in an occupied country.

Collaboration is a deceptively easy value to espouse. Almost everyone is engaged in some form of collaborative activity. To buy food in a supermarket requires the collaboration of farmers, factory workers, truck drivers, and a host of others ending with the clerk at the cash register or the person who bags the groceries. Whether we are purchasing products, receiving services, or just sitting in the sunshine in a public park, we enjoy benefits which are the result of people working together for a common purpose or a common goal. Collaboration must be a highly regarded value in our society.

Yes and no. People respect collaborative efforts, but competition is more highly regarded. Even a casual analysis of this society reveals how consistently we are encouraged to value and promote competition, from proponents of capitalism to participants in amateur and professional sports. We speak of the best man winning (even if that's a woman) and we argue that the most qualified person should get the promotion. We believe that the best companies ought to make the most money and the best workers should be paid the best salaries. The only exception to the rule is the recent trend of Americans questioning the large salaries paid to the best athletes. Given our history of racism, does this apparent inconsistency stem from the fact that a significant percentage of the best athletes today are people of color?

> **Competition**—striving to outdo another for acknowledgment, a prize, supremacy, profit . . . to engage in a contest, to struggle, rivalry.

Americans want to know who is the best professional football team in the country so we have a Super Bowl. We want to know who makes the most money so we have the Forbes 500. We are regularly informed of the top ten most popular songs and television programs and movies; we are provided with lists of people considered best dressed, most attractive, most popular; we give awards to individuals who make outstanding contributions in their field. In these and many more ways, we constantly celebrate individual achievement.

Collaboration occasionally makes a token appearance. At the Heisman Trophy ceremony to honor the best player in college football, a running back or quarterback may thank his offensive line; at the Academy Awards the Best Actress may thank everyone who worked on the film. These comments merely enhance the appeal of the recipients who are perceived not only as the best at what they do but also appealingly modest. Why do we promote this competition to outdo others? It required excellent performances from the entire football team to win the championship, but the quarterback receives the most valuable player award. Why do we continue to give awards for individual achievement even when the context for the achievement is a collaborative one?

There are many reasons, but perhaps the most compelling one is that competition provides us with two simple categories for perceiving people: winners and losers. There is no difficulty understanding who is to be admired. The results of competition are usually unambiguous, whereas collaboration is more muddled. In a group effort we can't always be certain what each person contributed to the final outcome. We don't know if everyone contributed equally or if some took credit while making minimal contributions. Collaboration forces us to operate in a world of uncertainty and ambiguity.

Another problem with collaboration is the necessity of compromise. For any collaboration to be successful, each participant usually makes concessions of some kind so the group can achieve its goal. Compromise means *resolving differences by making mutual concessions,* but the same term is used when someone makes *dishonorable or shameful concessions.* The second definition reveals the cause of our uneasiness with collaboration—each of us must determine at what point the concessions become dishonorable or shameful. At what point would I say I have compromised myself?

The definitions for collaboration reflect this concern by referring to a particularly shameful example of collaboration—those who cooperated with the Nazis during World War II. The heart of the dilemma in both collaboration and compromise is that we must make judgments about when our collaboration begins to compromise our principles such that continuing the collaboration would constitute a betrayal. It is a question of conscience. Competition is much more attractive. Collaboration is subjective, but competition is objective. Rather than identify ourselves as part of a group, we view ourselves as individuals testing our talents against others. We want the rewards awarded to the victors and the opportunity to try again if we fail, but we will be judged on our own merits.

The simplicity of competition is the reason it seems so satisfying. Individual achievements have always been important. Frequently an individual has had to challenge the collective belief of a community or society to be a catalyst for needed change. We celebrate and ought to celebrate these triumphs. What we fail to celebrate is the equal importance of ongoing collaborative activity in our daily lives. Every individual who has confronted the community has not always been right, and some have taken their followers down paths of pain and destruction resulting in unspeakable human misery.

Although it can be a perilous path, collaboration is the best way to ensure that everyone's needs are being met. Some people will resist collaboration to solve the problems of others because they are not directly suffering the consequences of the problem. In such cases, people have been forced to collaborate, as in the story above taken from Susan B. Anthony's favorite speech. As long as the poor had no power, those in power made little effort to respond to their needs. Once the poor were given the power of voting, even the leaders most opposed to giving assistance to the poor recognized the necessity for making sure that they and their children would be educated appropriately so they might use that power wisely. Cynics could argue that the real purpose of education being supported by the powerful in this instance was to ensure that the poor voted the way those in power wanted them to vote, but that merely illustrates how mixed motives create complexity in collaborative efforts.

Collaboration may force people to accept some uncertainty, but the certainty of competition can be as destructive as it is rewarding. Both parents and teachers need to nurture the qualities that contribute to success in collaborative activity. We need to appreciate the difficulty and the importance of negotiating compromises to create a common purpose. We should continue to celebrate individual achievements while recognizing the collaborative efforts behind those achievements. When we gaze in awe at the pyramids, we should remember not only the pharaohs buried there, but the thousands of ordinary workers who labored to produce such extraordinary monuments to collaborative activity.

### ₹₰ ₹₰ ₹₰
### *HEARING VOICES*

*When the best leaders' work is done,*
*the people say, "We did it ourselves!"*
Lao-Tzu

*Government and co-operation are in all*
*things the laws of life; anarchy and*
*competition the laws of death.*
John Ruskin

*The legitimate object of government is
to do for a community of people
whatever they need to have done, but
cannot do at all, in their separate and
individual capacities.*

Abraham Lincoln

*I am the inferior of any man whose rights
I trample underfoot.*

Horace Greeley

*I sit on a man's back, choking him and
making him carry me, and yet assure
myself and others that I am very sorry for
him and wish to ease his lot by all
possible means—except by getting off
his back.*

Alexis de Tocqueville

*When the head aches, all the members
share the pain.*

Miguel de Cervantes

*The greatest happiness of the greatest
number is the foundation of morals and
legislation.*

Jeremy Bentham

*We are quick enough in perceiving and
weighing what we bear from others;
but we think little of what others bear
from us.*

Thomas a. Kempis

*Come from where it may, racism
divides.*

Jose Marti

*Alone we can do so little; together we
can do so much.*

Helen Keller

*The era of force must give way to that of
knowledge, and the policy of the future
will be to teach and lead.*

Henry Gannett

*Corporations have neither bodies to be punished, nor souls to be condemned, they therefore do as they like.*

Edward, Baron Thurlow

*If all mankind minus one were of one opinion, and only one person were of the contrary opinion, mankind would be no more justified in silencing that one person, than he, if he had the power, would be justified in silencing mankind.*

John Stuart Mill

*For an idea ever to be fashionable is ominous, since it must afterwards be always old-fashioned.*

George Santayana

*Every generation laughs at the old fashions but religiously follows the new.*

Henry David Thoreau

*The foolish and the dead alone never change their opinion.*

James Russell Lowell

*To live is to change, and to be perfect is to have changed often.*

Cardinal Newman

*There is no higher religion than human service. To work for the common good is the greatest creed.*

Albert Schweitzer

*Until the great mass of the people shall be filled with the sense of responsibility for each other's welfare, social justice can never be attained.*

Helen Keller

*Where there is no vision, the people perish.*

Proverbs (28:18)

# WAS ORWELL WRONG?

The brief article in the newspaper reported that a black woman had marched into the local welfare office with a handgun, taken three hostages, and demanded an increase in her welfare payments. She said she could not get a job, and she could not raise three children on a monthly welfare check of slightly more than $200. After surrendering to authorities, she was taken to a mental hospital for psychiatric testing. Apparently the authorities were concerned that the poor woman was suffering from a mental illness.

In our society, this woman appears crazy not only to the authorities but probably to most of the people who read the article, but how many of them could raise three children on that amount of money? This mother was angry, not mad. It is the sanity of a society which creates such an inadequate welfare system that ought to be questioned.

In his novel *1984*, George Orwell described a future society in which the people who had the power eavesdropped on encounters, corrupted basic concepts, and manipulated minds under the watchful gaze of Big Brother, the archetypal bully [2]. Since the book's publication in 1948, social and political commentators in democratic societies have used Orwell's dystopia to warn of Machiavellian leaders and to denounce certain forms of government regulation as a treacherous ploy to intrude more deeply into our private lives. Should we be worried? If we had the power to see beyond the present, what kind of future awaits us? Optimists foresee a continuation of democratic societies with their promises of individual freedom and opportunity, but pessimists predict the rise of pseudo-democracies with highly regimented societies in which individuals feel alienated in an environment of suspicion and hostility.

It has been many years since we passed the 1984 milestone. Democratic societies have survived. Soviet state socialism is dead. We should feel much safer. Do we? In the United States there are indications that an ideology of alienation continues to evolve, creating such hostility and fear as to make Big Brother's machinations appear clumsy by comparison.

I developed a workshop on prejudice and discrimination for a group of police officers in a small Midwestern city. With the exception of one white female, the audience consisted exclusively of white males. In designing the workshop, I combined lecture information with a series of discussion activities where the officers could express their opinions. They listened politely and cooperated in the discussion activities but the anger was building. After an hour, the carefully designed activities gave way to a free-wheeling confrontation.

The men questioned and denied the severity, even the existence of discrimination against minorities and women. When I tried to talk about the history of discrimination in this society they rejected that as irrelevant, arguing "that was then, this is now." I offered to present them with current data comparing blacks and whites with regard to employment, promotions, and salary; the officers rejected this, arguing that statistics can be manipulated to prove anything. For the police officers at this workshop, the only acceptable basis for our dialogue was personal experience, and almost everyone had a story about a woman or a black man who had been the beneficiary of reverse discrimination. In each case the recipient was described as incompetent, as someone who should not have had the job or the promotion and who would not have had it without affirmative action policies. They appeared to know of no situations where a qualified woman or person of color was hired because of affirmative action policies, only cases where incompetent women or minorities were hired. They believed it was so; therefore, it was so.

The ideology which formed the foundation for the beliefs of these police officers did not spring fully formed from the head of Zeus. We can trace its origins and development as being concurrent with the development of the American work ethic and the American Dream, but the original meaning of the American Dream has been perverted into serving not as inspiration to all Americans, but as a rationalization for denying the role of prejudice and discrimination in subverting the American Dreams of oppressed people.

An example of this subversion is found in the cliche: *where there's a will, there's a way.* On the surface we have a motivational message intended to inspire people to work hard to achieve their goals. This advice is usually offered with confidence, as if it were a gold coin guaranteeing success, but there is another side to this coin. The assurance that hard work will always be rewarded by success suggests that those who have failed have only themselves to blame. The logic of this belief requires the believer to perceive poverty as proof of an individual's lack of determination, as an indisputable indicator of an inferior will.

Rejecting poor people as failures and as lesser human beings can be traced back to European antecedents. This is not to suggest that non-European countries were better or worse in their attitudes toward the poor than other countries around the world, but it is relevant to examine European attitudes toward poverty and impoverished people if we want to develop a context for understanding such attitudes in the United States. Here's a history lesson.

The responsibility of responding to the needs of poor people was largely a matter for the church from the time Constantine converted to Christianity, but the thirteenth and fourteenth centuries were times of turmoil and economic crises creating ever larger numbers of people in poverty. Something had to be done. In the sixteenth century, Henry VIII of England, regarded as one of the most enlightened monarchs of Europe, confronted the problem creatively. Henry made poverty a crime. The first time someone was arrested for being poor, meaning a transient with no money, that person was branded with a "V" for Vagrant. For the second offense of being poor, the criminal was forced to become an indentured servant for a fixed period of years. At the end of the allotted time the person would be released with the proper papers and possibly a little money if the servant had managed to save anything from the meager compensation received. For the third offense of being poor, the obviously unrepentant criminal was hanged. Thousands were hanged. Thus, Henry VIII conducted a war on poverty [3].

I believe many Americans continue to hold derogatory views of the poor, perceiving them as losers whose failure is rooted in their lack of determination to succeed. One of my colleagues visited a high school English class to observe a student teacher working with juniors as they discussed Harper Lee's novel *To Kill a Mockingbird* [4]. The nervous young teacher had run out of questions ten minutes before the end of class. My colleague could see desperation in his eyes. To ease his panic and because she was curious about the students' attitudes, she asked the student teacher if she could make a comment about the novel. She wanted to know if the students in the class would agree or disagree. The student teacher was happy to cooperate.

My colleague asked the students if they perceived the Ewell family as bad people and the Cunninghams as good people. Several nodded and a few rolled their eyes, presumably because the question seemed simplistic for someone who was supposed to be a college professor. She went on to say that there was another way to look at these two families which might be interesting to consider. The students did not look interested, but she persisted. Although both families were poor, the Cunninghams believed that no one else should worry about whether they had food or shelter or could take care of other needs. They would take care of themselves. Other people had no responsibility for helping them or anyone else who was poor. In contrast, the behavior of the Ewell family more accurately reflected the misery of poverty. She wondered if perhaps the students liked the Cunninghams because this family gave them a reason to ignore the problems of people living in poverty, and that was a message they wanted to hear.

After a moment of stunned silence, the students launched into a debate with this professor which revealed the extent of their hostility toward poor people. The theme of their comments was that if people were poor they deserved to be poor and we should not feel sorry for them. After much discussion one exasperated student wondered if the professor had ever talked to poor people, "Maybe they like being poor." When this student was asked if she really thought it was possible to enjoy living in dangerous and deteriorating housing, not having enough to eat, and fearing violence every day, she hesitated, momentarily uncertain. Her uncertainty was probably temporary. These students had been taught to blame the victim in so many ways for so many years that they could not separate the rationalization from reality. When the class ended, the students asked the professor if she would come back the next day. They were upset that they had not yet convinced her that they were right.

Poor people are not the only source of hostility and disparagement. Blaming the victim has long been practiced with women. The headline of a story in the local paper read "Skinny Dipper Charges Rape." With the information provided by the local police, the following facts were reported in the story:

1. The woman left a bar with two men sometime after midnight.
2. They drove to a beach on the river and went skinny dipping.
3. Later the woman had oral sex with one of the men.

Although the two men were friends, the man who was not involved in the oral sex came up behind his friend and knocked him unconscious; then he threw the woman into the back of his van and raped her. Her screams were heard by an airport security guard in the vicinity and as he arrived on the scene the woman was thrown out of the van. She was screaming that she had been raped. The guard heard an engine start and watched as the van drove off. Although there appeared to be ample evidence that a rape had occurred, the sensationalistic headline and the sexual details published in the paper made it unlikely that the woman could get a conviction for the man who raped her.

A few days later a friend of mine was at a social event on campus. She was not certain how men might respond to this issue, so she joined a group of women who were talking. During a pause in their discussion, she asked if anyone had seen the newspaper account of the "skinny dipper rape." Before she could express her concerns about how the victim was portrayed, one woman said, "Yes, I read that. She sure was asking for it!" As the other women nodded in agreement, my friend asked if any of them knew any woman who wanted to be raped. The outspoken woman became uncomfortable as my friend criticized the press for their use of inappropriate details in the newspaper article. After she finished, the outspoken women just shook her head and walked away. The remaining women made a few responses, but the issue was soon dropped. A week later the paper reported that the district attorney did not plan to prosecute unless additional evidence was provided. The testimony of the victim and two witnesses was apparently inadequate. The case never came to court.

Such cases don't come to court because we convict people in the court of public opinion, and the defendant does not get a chance to provide a defense. At a national education conference I participated in a roundtable discussion on the benefits of multicultural education. When our time was up most of the people drifted away except for a few who wanted to continue the conversation. A white woman described herself as a liberal and an advocate for multicultural education because she taught in an urban area. She was also concerned about adolescent *Chicanas* in her school district. Too many became pregnant and dropped out of school, some as young as fourteen. When I asked why this was happening, she claimed the girls were anxious to start a family whether they had a husband or not. If they did not have a husband they went on welfare. The woman believed drastic measures were necessary to resolve the problem: "I don't think I'm prejudiced, but the only solution I can see is sterilization." After a moment of stunned silence came a barrage of questions.

In response, the woman agreed that most of these young *Chicanas* faced common problems: they had difficulty with English; they had few or no marketable skills; they had little or no hope of employment even if they graduated from high school. She was also aware that most of the jobs available to these girls would involve subsistence wages with little chance for advancement. As the conversation ended, I had the impression that her advocacy of sterilization as a solution was still firm. Such "final solutions" may differ depending on the issue, but prejudices providing fertile ground for such solutions are widely held in America today. These prejudices are not limited to race and ethnicity and gender, but include religion and sexual orientation and people with disabilities and people with a mental illness and many other groups of people who struggle to survive in our diverse society.

Prejudices are reinforced by superficial media coverage, segregated neighborhoods, and by schools careless of their calling to nurture the best in our children and youth. If our nation is ever to become a collaborative community constantly creating and recreating ourselves based on a shared vision of what we want to be, we must confront prejudices and the negative behavior they cause before we deteriorate further into a society of warring camps more alienated, more frightened and more frightening than any Orwellian nightmare. Teachers have classrooms and curricula which should provide a safe place for students to question assumptions, challenge conclusions, and explore alternatives to inhumane "final solutions."

Although Orwell was wrong in his vision of Big Brother's crude methods of manipulation, he was correct in some of the details, as when he wrote "If thought corrupts language, language can also corrupt thought." We must look closely at words and phrases, in the media and elsewhere, for reports skewed to shape readers' reactions. People with disabilities being described as "confined" to a wheelchair reinforces the perception of people with a disability as limited rather than liberated by technology. I know a woman who is paraplegic. Without her wheelchair she might be "confined" to her bed, or at least to her house, but in her wheelchair she is mobile. She can go to her job, cruise the mall, attend the theater, and participate in as many activities as she chooses. She still faces problems, like the lack of curb cuts in certain places, but her wheelchair gives her freedom not confinement.

Years ago the phrase "special interests" referred to corporations and banks and powerful organizations using their power to influence politicians to pass laws favorable to their financial interests, but more recently that phrase has been used to describe people of color, women, labor unions, gay men and lesbians, and other groups of people who struggle to be heard in our society, who demand their civil rights as citizens in our democracy. Students should analyze language that demeans or demonizes those who are different.

This is especially important with regard to the labels, both formal and informal, given to groups of people. Whether the label is an obvious pejorative like "spic" or a bureaucratic label like "handicapped," we need to be aware of the power of such labels to stereotype individuals based on their differences. Students could learn much by looking at the origins of such words, for example the term "kike." Many immigrants to the United States have not been literate, and they would sign the immigration forms by simply making a mark. For Christians the mark was a cross or an X which resembled a cross. Because many Jewish immigrants came to the United States to escape religious persecution, they made a circle on the forms as their mark to ensure that they were not mistaken for Christians. The word circle in Yiddish is *kikel* which the immigrants would pronounce to the immigration officers as they made their distinctive mark. From a simple desire to have one's difference acknowledged and respected comes this insulting label used to denigrate Jews as a people [5, p. 249].

It is important to learn the lessons of labeling. A colleague told me of an incident that occurred during World War II while she was living in Seattle. Everyone was aware that the government was planning to relocate Japanese Americans away from the west coast and Asian Americans also knew they all looked alike to most white people. This presented entrepreneurs with a unique opportunity. Various buttons were manufactured proclaiming one's ethnic identity: "I am Chinese" or "I am Filipino" or "I am Korean." The buttons were not necessary for authorities charged with the responsibility of evacuating Japanese Americans because they would use official records to identify the people they wanted. The buttons were to help white people distinguish between the people they were supposed to hate and those who were acceptable. No buttons were worn by white Seattle residents to announce their non-German ancestry.

An Eskimo man came to one of the Seattle stores selling these buttons and asked for one that said "I am Eskimo." The merchant couldn't find such a button, and finally the merchant asked the customer to help him search through all of the buttons he had, but they were unable to find one with the Eskimo identification. Finally the customer purchased a button for each of the other Asian groups and wore all of them to ensure that he would not be mistaken for a Japanese American. The buttons became essential and they were worn by other Asian Americans every day until Japanese Americans were finally evacuated from Seattle.

Such stories should be told to students so they can examine alternate views of social issues and human conflict in history and literature. In schools they can stand away from the heat of battle and analyze the dehumanizing influences which are barriers to embracing a vision of our nation which is as dynamic and diverse as its people. Our best hope is that such discussions take students beyond the limitations of place and time to a future where we establish an awareness of the connections that bind us to one another, an awareness of the similarities that we share, an awareness of the differences that make us special. This awareness could be the basis for an authentic collaboration which can begin to create a community of trust. It could be the realization of an American Dream in which everyone participates. It is a dream worth pursuing. It is that pursuit which is described in the Brazilian proverb:

When we dream alone, we merely dream;
When we dream together, that is the beginning of reality.

## ❧ ❧ ❧
## *ECHOES*

*This country will not be a good place
for any of us to live in unless we
make it a good place for all of us
to live in.*

Theodore Roosevelt

*It is largely up to the politicians which
social forces they choose to liberate, and
which they choose to suppress, whether
they rely on the good in each citizen or
on the bad . . . it is their responsibility to
seek out the best in that society, and to
develop it and strengthen it.*

Vaclav Havel

*The role of the teacher remains the
highest calling of a free people. To
the teacher, America entrusts her most
precious resource, her children; and
asks that they be prepared, in all their
glorious diversity, to face the rigors
of individual participation in a
democratic society.*

Shirley Hufstedler

*If I had a child who wanted to be a
teacher, I would bid him Godspeed as if
he were going to war. For the war
against prejudice, greed and ignorance
is eternal, and those who dedicate
themselves to it give their lives no less
because they may live to see some
fraction of the battle won.*

James Hilton

*The one real object of education is
to have individuals in the condition
of continually asking questions.*

Bishop Mandell Creighton

*We must have towns that accommodate
different educational groups, different
economic groups, different ethnic
groups, towns where all can live in
one place.*

Margaret Mead

*Every gun that is made, every warship
launched, every rocket fired signifies,
in the final sense, a theft from those
who hunger and aren't fed, those
who are cold and are not clothed.*

Dwight D. Eisenhower

*A nation that continues year after year
to spend more money on military
defense than on programs of social
uplift is approaching spiritual death.*

Martin Luther King, Jr.

*The one thing that doesn't abide by
majority rule is a person's conscience.*

Harper Lee

*Many people consider the things which
government does for them to be social
progress, but they consider the things
government does for others as
socialism.*

Earl Warren

*We can have a democracy in this country
or we can have great wealth in the hands
of a few, but we can't have both.*

Louis Brandeis

*No one can go it alone. Somewhere
along the way is the person who gives
you that job, who has faith that you
can make it.*

Grace Gil Olivarez

*When you do nothing, you feel
overwhelmed and powerless. But when
you get involved, you feel the sense
of hope and accomplishment that
comes from knowing you are working
to make things better.*

Pauline R. Kezer

*In one of our concert grand pianos,
243 taut strings exert a pull of 40,000
pounds on an iron frame. It is proof that
out of great tension may come great
harmony.*

Theodore Steinway

*I should like to be able to love my
country and to love justice.*

Albert Camus

*Everyone likes to give as well as to
receive. No one wishes only to receive
all the time. We have taken much from
your culture . . . I wish you had taken
something from our culture for there
were some good and beautiful things
in it.*

Chief Dan George

# THE ONLY GOOD INDIAN . . . IS A MASCOT

> . . . as a counterpart to the Redskins, we need an NFL team called
> "Niggers" to honor Afro-Americans. Half-time festivities for fans
> might include a simulated stewing of the opposing coach in a large
> pot while players and cheerleaders dance around it, garbed in
> leopard skins and wearing fake bones in their noses. . . . (Hispanics)
> can be "represented" by the Galveston "Greasers" and San Diego
> "Spics" . . . Asian Americans? How about the "Slopes," "Dinks,"
> "Gooks," . . . Let's see. Who's been left out? Teams like the Kansas
> City "Kikes" . . . Dayton "Dagos" and Pittsburgh "Polacks" will fill a
> certain social void among white folk [6, pp. 414-415].

In this satirical quotation, Ward Churchill asks that we take a trivial
issue seriously, which suggests it may not be so trivial. He's right.
There's nothing trivial about labeling people as "redskins" any more
than we can dismiss such references as "niggers" or "kikes" as trivial.
These are powerful, derisive words. They damage those who use them
and those who are labeled by them. To continue using a reference as
offensive as *redskins* is to persist in an inexcusable act of demeaning an
entire race of people. That, by definition, is racist.

Some people might accept Churchill's argument in the case of
extreme examples but deny that such a racist message exists in
references such as Indians, Braves, or Warriors because these names
were given to sports teams in admiration of the fighting spirit of Indian
warriors. Even if the names are intended to honor Indians and show
respect for them, they present a problem because they represent a
stereotype. There is no human being who can be legitimately labeled
"the Indian." There were and are a variety of culturally distinct groups
of Indians, or Native Americans, in the United States.

At the time Columbus landed on these shores there were about
500 nations [7]—each with cultural differences reflected in language,
lifestyle, housing, religion. There were societies based on farming,
fishing, trading, and hunting/gathering. There were stable societies
that stayed in one place and nomadic societies that followed the game.
There were Seminoles sleeping under a chiki, Apaches coming home to
their wikiups, Navajos eating in their hogans, Kwakiutl gathering in
their heida houses, and Lakota moving about in their portable tipis.
Such diversity can never be represented by a single term like Indian.
The term and the stereotype is based on the Plains Indians—
hunter/gatherers, mounted warriors, nomads. This is the conventional
stereotype for Indians which has been used in film and fiction and in
educational materials since "I is for Indian" first appeared below an

image of a Native American in a full headdress in books teaching children the alphabet, and a lot more than the alphabet.

Such references also taught children that Indian people were part of the past—as much an historical artifact as the arrowheads still found here and there during spring plowing. *A long time ago and far away lived the Indians:*

> by the shores of Gitchee Gummie
> by the shining big sea waters [8, p. 2].

The noble savage lived on the land in harmony with nature until he was tragically overwhelmed by the *Manifest Destiny* of white colonization. It was nobody's fault. It was fate. Now they're gone. Let's shed a tear and then go to a game and whoop and stomp and do the tomahawk chop and "How about those Atlanta Braves!" (Just showing respect for the dearly departed.)

But Native Americans are not gone. They do not merely belong to the past but live in the present. For many, that life is a struggle, a fight for quality of life on several levels, but it is a struggle that is ongoing. It would be helpful if more non-Indians understood the problems faced by Indians on the reservations and in urban areas. It would be helpful if those in power showed respect for contemporary Indians and concern for their problems. It would be helpful if the non-Indian people would work with Indian people to solve these problems. Instead non-Indian children learn only about Indians who lived in the past.

When my daughter was in elementary school one of her best friends was a girl who belonged to a tribe called Winnebago but who called themselves Ho Chunk. One day in school the children were reading about Indians and my daughter's friend informed her classmates that she was an Indian. The children refused to believe her even though she was darker than any of them and had straight black hair like the Indians in their pictures. She couldn't be an Indian because she wore clothes like theirs, talked like them, played like them. They could not be convinced that she was an Indian because she didn't fit the stereotypical images in their books. The children had learned their lessons well.

Indian mascots reinforce the lesson of the Indian as an artifact of history. Look at the human mascots used by sports teams: pirates and buccaneers, vikings and raiders, knights and lancers, Trojans and Spartans, cowboys and Indians. These are all people we associate with the past, not the present. In cases where one could imagine a more contemporary image like the "Fighting Irish," the mascot is a leprechaun which visually distances the meaning of the mascot from any notion of contemporary Irish people.

Imagine the scene—it's the Indians playing the Panthers in the big football game of the season. At the pep rally before the game, a Native American father whose son is the Panthers' starting wide receiver brings his younger children to witness the excitement of the pre-game activities. During the pep rally the students begin shouting "Kill the Indians!" and "Scalp the Indians!" followed by "war whoops" and blood curdling yells. The Indian children become frightened and turn to their father, "Why do they want to kill us daddy?" Later at the game the Indian children see someone in a Panther costume prowling up and down the sideline on one side of the field and someone (probably white) with a painted face and pseudo-Indian attire pacing up and down on the other side. What are they to make of this? The Native American father who told me this story did not have to imagine it. He was there. He had to explain it to his children.

When people say the Indian mascot is to show honor and respect, they mean it is intended to respect Indians as fighters, but the use of animals for mascots illustrates the real meaning of such respect. Lions and tigers and panthers are selected as mascots because they are seen as savage killers who hunt weaker animals and kill them for food. It is their ferociousness that is admired and they are used as a mascot to suggest that the sports team embodies a similar kind of ferociousness in their approach to the game. This association of Indians with animals implies the notion of savagery which was used for years as the justification for exterminating Indians. "The only good Indian is a dead Indian." Remember? Indian history is replete with stories of whites engaged in barbarous acts of treachery, betrayal, and monstrous cruelty inflicted on Indians because they were perceived as savages and brute beasts and even subhuman. Is it any wonder that so many Native Americans have protested the use of Indian mascots?

Although there appears to be wide agreement among Native Americans that Indian mascots are unacceptable and demeaning, there is not unanimous agreement. This is not surprising. It is impossible to have unanimous agreement from any diverse group on any controversial issue. White people do not refuse to take action on an issue because not all whites are in agreement, yet many whites will use the opinions of those Native Americans who say they are not offended by Indian mascots as their justification for not eliminating them.

Another tactic used to resist changing Indian mascots is to appeal to the majority. While students at a Midwestern university were embroiled in a difficult debate over whether or not to eliminate the school's Indian mascot, the local newspaper took a poll of their readers asking if they thought the mascot was offensive. Over 90 percent responded that it was not offensive to them, and over 90 percent of the readers were white. Of course it wasn't offensive to them. That's part of the problem, and such a survey is not the way to find a solution.

Ultimately this is an issue about power. White people selected Indian mascots, are attached to these mascots and want to keep them. When Native Americans explain why it is offensive to them, most whites become almost apoplectic about what an honor the mascot represents. Such comments can reach the height of absurdity as happened during one university's debate over their mascot. The Native American Student Association on the campus made a public statement that they were opposed to retaining the Indian mascot. Shortly after this, a white male wrote to the editor of the local newspaper insisting that the Indian mascot was an honor and demonstrated how much whites respected Indians. As for the opposition of Native American students, the letter writer insisted that any Indians who didn't agree with his point of view "didn't deserve to be called an Indian." This white male was claiming the right to designate who should be regarded as a real Indian. And remember, he respected real Indians.

White people who claim that Indian mascots symbolize honor and respect for Indians often make comments revealing their lack of respect for the opinions of contemporary Native Americans. This juxtaposition illustrates one scholar's contention that most white people have a dual perspective concerning Indians [9]. On the one hand is the Noble Savage portrayed as a spiritual being who lived in harmony with nature and was a courageous warrior who tried to protect his family and his doomed way of life. The other image is of degraded Indians, corrupted by alcohol and white men's ways, disconnected from their heritage and history. Nothing noble here. Nothing worthy of respect.

If whites and others who are not Indian want to demonstrate respect for Indians, they must listen to contemporary Native Americans and respond to what they have to say. If non-Indians want to provide evidence that they honor Indians, they must honor the feelings of contemporary Native Americans and not merely the distorted memory of Indians in the past. If non-Indians really want to honor Indians, they need to hear what is being said as Native Americans explain why they are NOT honored by Indian mascots. They need to understand how the dances and symbols mocked by mascots are part of the historic, religious beliefs of many Indians, part of their sense of the sacred.

How would Christians of all colors feel if a team calling itself Christians had a mascot dressed like Christ (with a crown of thorns and fake blood flowing from his hands and feet) who patrolled the sidelines and did cartwheels every time there was a score? What if a team calling itself the Muslims had a mascot called Muhammed who rode a horse up and down the sidelines shrieking "Kill the infidel" and waving a scimitar over his head? If such mascots would offend Christians and Muslims, then we should understand why Native Americans are offended.

Some white people resist changing an Indian mascot by saying "Why should we change it? We are the majority and we should have the final say." Exactly. When students at a Midwestern university were considering the elimination of their Indian mascot, they announced a meeting to debate this issue. At the meeting, a panel of students of color explained why they supported the Native American students who wanted the mascot eliminated. Following the panel presentation, a white male student in the audience stood up and said that since the majority of students on the campus wanted to keep the Indian mascot, the mascot should remain. He did not mention the important fact that the majority of students were white, but an African American woman on the panel rose to her feet and said, "If the majority always got to have its way I'd still be sitting in the back of the bus back home in Alabama." Exactly.

As a last resort, I have heard some people try to avoid the issue by arguing that it's a trivial one compared to the alcohol problems, unemployment problems, and many other problems faced by Indians on reservations and elsewhere. They argue that we should be trying to solve these problems instead of wasting time on something as trivial as the mascot issue. In comparison to these problems, the mascot issue certainly seems trivial, but unlike the other problems, eliminating the Indian mascot is a simple and easy change. White people have the power to make this change immediately because white people are still the majority in the United States, at least for the moment. Eliminating Indian mascots would not require years of planning nor significant resources but could be done in a short time at minimal cost. If white people and others who are not Indian are not willing to change something as trivial as an Indian mascot, why should Native Americans believe these people when they say they have a genuine commitment to help solve the more complicated and damaging problems affecting Native Americans?

Eliminating Indian mascots may seem trivial, but it is a powerful symbol of people refusing to acknowledge racism. To refuse to listen to Native Americans on this issue is to betray a reluctance to share power in creating mutually acceptable solutions. The Indian mascot issue is a test of the degree to which non-Indians genuinely feel honor and respect for Indians. Are we going to eliminate Indian mascots? In the years ahead, how non-Indians respond to that question will not be seen as a trivial issue.

In a society as diverse as ours, the cohesiveness of its people can be determined by the response of a group with power to the concerns of other groups with less power. If white people listen to Native Americans on the mascot issue, understand what they are saying and respond appropriately, this will suggest that our society embraces collaboration over coercion, that we honor mutual decision making and not the tyranny of the majority. As John Howard Griffen said, "Rule by the majority is a great idea, but the majority has no right to rule wrong based on prejudice" [cited in 10, p. 311]. If our society, composed of so many different groups, is to be a unified nation, we must live and work and play and solve our conflicts together. If we do, we can realize the vision expressed in the motto: *e pluribus unum* . . . out of the many, one.

# CHAPTER FOUR
## In the Key of D:  DIVERSITY

### THE RESIGNATION

Jerry Winegar was born and raised in rural Kansas. As a boy growing up during the Eisenhower era he did not notice segregation, but in high school he became aware of the rigid separation of Black and White people. It didn't seem right. By the time he was in college the Civil Rights movement was gaining momentum. Winegar was inspired by the moral courage of Black people and the leadership of Martin Luther King, Jr. As a young teacher and coach, Jerry spent the 1960s discussing issues of social justice with his students, working for school desegregation and supporting the Civil Rights movement. Then Martin Luther King, Jr. was assassinated. Jerry was devastated. He resigned from his teaching position and enrolled at the college where he had already completed several courses during previous summers.

One of the professors at the college had been Jerry's mentor and was well aware of his commitments and his activism for civil rights. The professor was surprised to see Jerry on campus that fall, and asked him why he was there. Winegar talked about the assassination of King and his despair about the country resolving its racial problems. "I guess I just got tired," he concluded, "so I resigned from my job and came here to get my Master's Degree." The professor paused and then spoke quietly, "Do you suppose Black people get tired, Jerry? What do they resign from?" [1].

> **Diversity**—differing from one another, having various forms or qualities . . . unlike . . . multiformity. Antonyms are identical, selfsame.

The Hmong people did not willingly immigrate from Southeast Asia; they were forced out of their homes in the highlands of Laos, one of the consequences of the Vietnam war. Many Hmong are concerned about their culture changing radically or even disappearing as a result of the diaspora. At a presentation describing some of the unique beliefs and

73

practices in the Hmong culture, a Hmong man spoke with obvious pride about his cultural heritage. Afterwards a member of the audience asked the speaker to describe what the Hmong culture and American culture had in common. This sort of response often occurs when individuals from a racial or ethnic group talk about the unique features of their group. Although it is important to recognize the commonalities we share as human beings, it is also important to value our differences. In the United States, we still tend to regard anyone who is different with suspicion.

> **Conformity**—acting in accord or harmony with a standard or norm, agreement, congruity . . . being or becoming similar in form or character . . . compliance or acquiescence.

By contrast, conformity is encouraged in our society. People might not openly advocate conformity, but it is rewarded. Because of these rewards, the pressure to conform makes it more difficult for people to be advocates for the value of diversity. This is an interesting contradiction. America puts a high priority on individuality, yet there is enormous pressure to conform to cultural norms. America celebrates our freedom to make individual decisions, but those decisions can come at a high price if they are contrary to the expectations of the dominant culture. The desire for conformity is rooted in a desire for harmony. If all agree, there is no conflict; therefore, fear of conflict is one of the barriers to valuing diversity.

People mistakenly believe that differences inevitably lead to conflict. It is true that most friendships are formed from common interests, but once a friendship is formed, the differences between individuals sustain the relationship. This is not true in all cases because some people seek relationships where they are the focus and have the power. They want to be in control. The other person in the relationship is expected to conform to the partner's demands. But in a mutually satisfying relationship, people listen to each other, express concern for each other, and engage in mutual decision-making. They share power rather than strive for power over the other. In this kind of relationship, differences between the partners stimulate their continuing interest in each other, and their differences determine how their relationship evolves.

An appreciation for diversity is evident when people are asked to respond to this question: "Would you like to live in a society where everyone was the same?" At this basic level, people are attracted to diversity and most people of all ages say "No." They often add a comment about how boring it would be if we were all the same. A similar question produces the same response: "Would you like to live in a society where everyone was just like you?" If I like myself, the idea of everyone being just like me is initially appealing, but if everyone was just like me I would lose my individuality and be indistinguishable from other people. In a society which emphasizes individuality, this is not appealing.

These responses suggest why we should value diversity. If I value aspects of myself that make me different from others, then I should value those aspects in others that make them different from me. There are multiple factors shaping an individual's personality which is why each person is unique. If we would appreciate those factors, we could understand how much we have to learn from each other. When we are learning about others we learn about ourselves. If being white and male has helped to shape the positive feelings I have about myself, then race and gender are important factors to value. If someone is black and female, those factors have shaped her individuality and I should acknowledge and respect that. If we explore our differences, we will become intimately entangled in the complexity that is our human heritage.

Human heritage is multicultural, but we have tended to segregate it, especially in schools. We have separated the white experience in our history, literature, and the arts and presented that to students as the American experience. When people of color demand that a more accurate and inclusive experience be presented in schools, many whites have seen this as self-serving; they do not realize that they have as much to gain by promoting diversity as people of color. With a society as diverse as ours, all of us are enriched by hearing the different voices and by understanding the perspectives of individuals from diverse groups. Knowing what people of color have contributed to our society also creates a sense of unity. We are a nation of diverse groups who share the responsibility for what this nation has been and is becoming.

Although people of color have a clearer motivation for promoting the goal of respecting differences, that does not make the goal irrelevant to whites. As illustrated in Jerry Winegar's story, white people have the option of choosing whether or not to be involved in the struggle to create a society that values its diversity. Some white people have opposed such efforts from a mistaken sense that it is in their self-interest to maintain the status quo, but even white people benefit from a society that values and celebrates diversity. The British author G. K. Chesterton recognized that a century ago:

> It is a great mistake to suppose that love unites and unifies men. Love diversifies them, because love is directed towards individuality. The thing that really unites men and makes them like to each other is hatred . . . the more we hate Germany the more we shall copy German guns and German fortifications in order to be armed against Germany. The more modern nations detest each other the more meekly they follow each other; for all competition is in its nature only a furious plagiarism. As competition means always similarity, it is equally true that similarity always means inequality. If everything is trying to be green, some things will be greener than others; but there is an immortal and indestructible equality between green and red [2, pp. 179-180].

Although it is important to affirm the common concerns that unite us, we need to appreciate the differences between us as well, and not just physical differences like skin color. We need to listen to ideas whether we agree with them or not, and try to understand why someone might believe ideas so different from our own. Understanding different perspectives can promote harmony between individuals and groups without requiring conformity of thought. To achieve this goal, it is essential to debate ideas without attacking the person who offers them. To value diversity means to celebrate individuality by recognizing how individuality is shaped by life experiences influenced by membership in diverse groups. Valuing diversity results in respect not only for individuals within a diverse nation but, as Chesterton said, it creates respect between nations. As communication and trade and travel bring the different peoples of the world closer together, we need to understand the differences between us if we are to create or maintain respect for one another.

### HEARING VOICES

*We are all citizens of one world; we are all of one blood. To hate someone because he was born in another country because he speaks a different language, or because he takes a different view on a subject, is a great folly.*

John Comenius

*(Prejudice) is a tyrant of the human
mind, which rushes on its prey through a
thousand avenues almost as soon as men
begin to think and feel, and which seldom
relinquishes its iron sway until they cease
to do either. . .*

James Fenimore Cooper

*Prejudices, it is well known, are most
difficult to eradicate from the heart
whose soil has never been loosened or
fertilized by education; they grow there,
firm as weeds among stones.*

Charlotte Bronte

*"My idea of an agreeable person," said
Hugo Bohum, "is a person who agrees
with me."*

Benjamin Disraeli

*It happened one time during a speech by
Phocion that the people suddenly began
applauding wildly. Phocion turned to one
of his friends and said, "Have I said
something foolish?"*

Diogenes Laertius

*It's always best on these occasions to
do what the mob do." "But suppose
there are two mobs?" suggested
Mr. Snodgrass. "Shout with the largest,"
replied Mr. Pickwick.*

Charles Dickens

*Man is a gregarious animal, and much
more so in his mind than in his body. He
may like to go alone for a walk, but he
hates to stand alone in his opinions.*

George Santayana

*Whoso would be a man must be a
nonconformist.*

Ralph Waldo Emerson

*It ain't the things we don't know that*
*makes such fools of us, but a whole lot of*
*things that we know that ain't so.*

Josh Billings

*People will love you if you make them*
*think they are thinking, but they will hate*
*you if you make them think.*

Voltaire

*Until lions have their historians, tales of*
*hunting will always glorify the hunter.*

African Proverb

*The best way to suppose what may come,*
*is to remember what is past.*

George Savile

*Progress, far from consisting in change,*
*depends on retentiveness . . . Those who*
*cannot remember the past are*
*condemned to fulfill it.*

George Santayana

*What experience and history teach is*
*this—that people and governments never*
*have learned anything from history, or*
*acted on principles deduced from it.*

G. W. F. Hegel

*Governments exist to protect the rights of*
*minorities. The loved and the rich need*
*no protection.*

Wendell Phillips

*It is in life as it is in ways, the shortest*
*way is commonly the foulest, and surely*
*the fairer way is not much about.*

Francis Bacon

*Virtue shuns ease as a companion. It*
*demands a rough and thorny path.*

Michel Montaigne

*The wise person can see a question from*
*all sides without bias. The foolish person*
*can see a question only from one side.*

Confucius

## IN THE LAND OF LIBERTY

*A Parable about the Separation of
Church and State*

(*Note:* This parable is not based upon a real country nor
is it intended as a completely accurate depiction
of Islamic beliefs and practices.)

Isaiah Maxwell Goodman was worried. When the opportunity was offered, Ike (as everyone called him) had thought it would be an adventure to relocate to the Middle East and give his family the experience of living in a foreign country with its different customs and traditions. His family embraced the idea with an enthusiasm that made Ike feel proud. There were practical advantages as well. The offer to relocate included a promotion and a substantial increase in salary, but this alone would not have tempted Ike to take the position. To assure himself that taking the position would be in the best interests of his family and not just a selfish decision to enhance his career, Ike had thoroughly researched this heretofore unknown Islamic nation. He had been impressed with what he read.

A growing American community was providing knowledge and skills needed for developing the resources of this small Muslim nation. The nation had a strong admiration for the United States and its democratic form of government. That admiration had promoted the creation and adoption of a Constitution modeled on that of the United States. The prosperity of their economy was obvious from the number of attractive homes and modern office buildings, the excellent roads, the efficient transportation system, and other developments characteristic of a modern, progressive society.

The American community had built churches of several different Christian denominations, but there were no separate schools for American children. Even this deficit was apparently not a problem since there were two elementary schools and a secondary school with English only immersion programs and high academic standards to attract local students interested in developing proficiency in English. American students were not only accommodated, they were welcomed into the immersion schools which were part of a system of state-supported schools. These state schools did not include required classes in the Islamic religion because their Constitution had a provision similar to our first amendment prohibiting the establishment of a state religion and guaranteeing religious freedom. There were private schools for Muslim parents who wanted their children to receive religious instruction in school.

Impressed with what he had read, Ike concluded that this promotion was a good opportunity for his family as well as himself. The country seemed to have earned the right to use its slogan, often quoted in tourist brochures and business advertisements: "The Land of Liberty."

The Goodman family moved in August. Despite the warm temperatures the entire family was excited about living in this strange new place. They worried a little about what adaptations they might have to make, but little adaptation seemed necessary. They had a beautiful home in a suburb of a bustling and growing urban area. Close to their home they found a mall with a movie theater complex featuring American films, a miniature golf course, even a MacDonald's. There was nothing to complain about until the children started attending school.

It began when their fifteen-year-old son told his parents that the Muslim students prayed twice during the school day. Jeff thought it was interesting how the Muslim students spread their prayer rugs on the floor and "when they kneel down to pray they're like, all facing the same direction and they bow down really low!" Ike smiled at Jeff's enthusiasm. "I talked to one of the guys and he said they were facing in the direction of the Ka'aba in Mecca, the holy city. Do you know what the Ka'aba is Dad? I didn't want him to think I was stupid so I didn't ask."

"Don't be afraid to ask, son. One of the reasons why we're here is to learn about another culture." Ike walked over to his bookshelf. "I remember reading about the Ka'aba. It's the most sacred building in all Islam and it contains a large black rock. Some people think the rock is a meteorite. This rock is considered so sacred that only Muslims are allowed to see it when they make their pilgrimage to Mecca." Ike had taken a book from the shelf and he handed it to Jeff. "You can read about it in here if you're interested."

"Maybe later." Jeff was not enthusiastic, but he took the book. "I've got a lot of homework to do, but there was one more thing that seemed sort of weird to me though."

"And that was?"

"Well, some American kids got down on their knees and prayed with the Muslim kids."

"I didn't think there were any Muslims among the American students."

"That's just it, there aren't any. That's why it was weird."

"Did you talk to any of them? Did you ask them why they did that?"

"I only talked to this one guy. I figured they were just goofing around or maybe they were real religious and wanted to pray since the school was taking time for prayer, but that wasn't what the guy said that I talked to. He just said it's better to go along if you want to get along."

Ike was slightly troubled by what Jeff said, but he shrugged it off.

A few weeks later Ike was troubled once again when Jeff mentioned that his literature teacher was reading aloud passages from the Qur'an and explaining the special relationship between Muhammed and God. Ike asked if the teacher was saying anything else about Islamic beliefs. According to Jeff the teacher had made a number of comments about Islamic beliefs from the creation of the world to the nature of the soul and the possibility of eternal life. Ike tried to rationalize that it was probably good for Jeff to develop some understanding of another religion, but he was still uncomfortable.

Ike had insisted that all his children attend Sunday School classes at the Lutheran church when they were children, and Jeff had attended church with his parents ever since he had been confirmed three years ago. Ike was confident that Jeff understood and accepted their faith, but he wanted to make sure Jeff would not become confused by what was happening at school. Ike told Jeff he wanted to meet with him once a week to read and discuss the Bible. Ike said it would be good for both of them.

Being sensitive to his position as a foreigner in this country, Ike tried to keep an open mind about the school situation, but Jeff continued to come home with examples of Islamic ideas and practices which intruded into the academic work. Ike began to get angry. The accumulating evidence began to convince him that the school was involved in a conscious and deliberate effort of religious indoctrination, not only of his children but of all Christian students in the school.

In addition to prayers, teachers often provided explanations of the Qur'an which sounded as if they were promoting Muslim beliefs in the classroom. In music class students had chanted passages from the Qur'an to selected music. Afterwards they shouted in unison "Muhammed is the messenger of God" and "There is no God but Allah!" School was dismissed for major Islamic holy days, but if the Christian students were absent from school on Christmas or Good Friday they were not excused and had to make up their assignments. During Ramadan, the star and crescent moon appeared on classroom walls and in the hallways; in class students participated in celebrations of the Muslim faith. All students were usually called together in the large assembly room to commemorate important events from Islamic history, these were often concluded by having the students recite passages from the Qur'an. When Christmas came, no nativity scene was displayed, not even a Christmas tree. No carols were sung.

Although Ike was disturbed by all of this, he wasn't sure what he could do about it. He had talked to some of the parents at his church, but they just shrugged and said they did not want to cause any trouble. For the past few weeks he thought about going to the headmaster to complain, but he resisted the temptation. He had resolved to make the best of it and to keep an open mind. Then the prayer issue came up again, and this time Ike had heard enough.

It happened during one of their Bible study sessions. Jeff seemed to have something on his mind, and finally he asked a question. "I was just kind of wondering . . . Do you think it would be all right if I prayed with the rest of the kids?" Jeff could tell from the look on his father's face that Ike didn't like the question, so he quickly went on. "See, I would pray to God like I always do, but I would just be doing it on my knees next to the Muslim kids. That wouldn't be wrong would it?"

Ike slowly shut the Bible in his hand. "Why do you want to do this?"

Jeff looked at the floor. "It's just that, well, there are only two or three Christian kids who don't take part in these prayers now. I mean, no one's forcing them to do it or anything, but that's the way it is."

"What do you mean? Why are the American kids doing this?"

"It's hard to explain. It's just . . . the Muslim kids treat you differently if you don't pray with them. I think maybe it's because so many of the American kids are praying with them so now it's sort of like they think you don't believe in God at all if you don't pray, or that you don't respect their religion or something."

"What do you mean, they treat you differently? What do they do?" As Jeff sat there, struggling for words, Ike wished his son was still a child so he could hug him and tell him that everything would be all right.

"I don't know it's . . . they don't pick on me or anything and they still seem to be friendly to me, but they also act a little more formal around the few of us who aren't praying with them than they do around the other Americans."

"The kids who are praying?"

"Yeah, and even the Americans who are praying seem to keep their distance from me and the others who don't pray, like they don't want to do anything to spoil things with the Muslim kids."

"I'm sorry to hear that, Jeff. As for this prayer business, there is nothing wrong with you praying to God when the Muslim students are saying their prayers. What bothers me is that you feel forced to pray, because I believe that prayers should be said when you have something to say to God and not when someone tells you to pray. But if it would help you to pray with the others then I guess that's what you should do." Ike opened the Bible to the page he had marked.

A weight seemed to lift from Jeff's shoulders. "Thanks. I know this will help. I didn't want to worry you, but I kind of got in a little trouble in literature class." Ike closed the Bible and waited for Jeff to continue. "The teacher was going on about how important it was to be a good Muslim and, I don't know, I just got tired of it. I said that there was nothing wrong with being a Christian and that it was just as good as being a Muslim."

"And what did the teacher say to that?"

"Well, he didn't disagree with me or anything, but he didn't ask anyone to say anything more about it. He just stopped that discussion and started talking about something else. After class none of the Muslim kids would talk to me. They just avoided me. They were always friendlier with the American kids who prayed with them, but now they're not saying anything to me. This has been going on for a couple of days, and I know I've got to do something. I'm hoping that if I start praying with them they will start talking to me again. I don't know what else to do."

Ike was furious. He said nothing about his feelings to Jeff, but he did ask his son to let him know if the situation at school got better or worse. That night Ike got little sleep or relief from his anger. The next morning he made an appointment with the school headmaster. Ike arrived promptly after lunch.

The headmaster introduced himself and offered Ike a chair. Ike quickly identified himself as a concerned parent and that what concerned him most was that the school was engaging in a form of religious indoctrination of his son and the other Christian students who attended the school. Ike read the list of the grievances he had written down. While he was reading from his list the headmaster listened calmly, never interrupting but with a puzzled look. When Ike finished his list of complaints, the headmaster cleared his throat before he spoke.

"Aren't you being a little harsh on us, Mr. Goodman? I don't believe it is fair to call what we do in this school religious indoctrination."

"Why not?" Ike's response sounded like an assertion more than a question.

"Well, for one thing our holy days are cultural as much as they are religious, so of course we acknowledge them in our school. Furthermore, it is just common sense to dismiss school on those days when the overwhelming majority of students would not be able to attend anyway since they would be involved in their religious celebrations. What would you have us do Mr. Goodman, deny our culture or the importance of Islam to our culture?

"No, I'm not suggesting that." Ike already felt defensive.

"And as for teaching the Qur'an," here he paused and leaned toward Ike, "it is a great and influential book in the annals of human history, is it not?"

"Well, I suppose it is, but that's not my point . . ."

"But that is exactly my point! What possible excuse would we have for not reading the Qur'an? It is essential for a sound understanding of our cultural beliefs and our literature. I have visited several schools in the United States and while I was there I examined some of your curricular materials. I have seen poetry from the Bible and some of the stories from the Bible in literature anthologies. It would appear that this religious material is taught in your schools. Do you agree that this is true?"

"I guess so," Ike spoke quickly now, "but I'm sure that when the Bible is taught in our schools it is *not* used to impose any particular set of beliefs on students."

"Neither do we, Mr. Goodman. My teachers simply explain the meaning of certain important passages in the Qur'an."

"Then why not teach what it says in the Bible, too?"

"Our teachers do not feel proficient in the teaching of comparative religion, and our students have not indicated much interest in this area. We tried to offer such a course a few years ago, but the students were too busy with their required subjects."

The conversation was not going the way Ike had hoped, so he tried a new tactic. "Well, I just think that if you're going to include all of these references to the Muslim faith, it is not too much to ask that there be some kind of recognition of the Christian faith as well."

"But we do Mr. Goodman!" The headmaster smiled broadly. "Ash Wednesday occurs near one of our major holy days, so we use that occasion to tell our students about Lent." Ike's glum expression made it clear that he was not appeased by this announcement. "I believe that is an appropriate gesture on our part and I am disappointed that you have not mentioned that."

"But what about . . ."

"Now just a minute sir." The headmaster's smile was replaced by a stern expression and a narrowing of his eyes. "I have let you speak; now it is my turn to respond to your complaints. You mention the holy verses chanted in music classes by our students. Once again I must remind you that these verses are not merely religious, they are part of our culture. I see no reason why we should not include important aspects of our culture in the school."

Ike interrupted, "But there is some beautiful music reflecting Christian beliefs, why not include that? Why not have students sing some Christian music at Christmas?"

The headmaster shook his head, "We are not well versed in Western musical traditions, except for the rock and roll which our students listen to on the radio." He smiled briefly, then resumed a serious expression. "I will talk to our music teacher about finding some appropriate Christian music if that's what you would like me to do. I am willing to be reasonable about this, but I must tell you something. Two years ago one of our music teachers tried to get the American students to teach us some Christian songs, but they seemed embarrassed and uncomfortable so we did not insist. We will be glad to ask them again if that would satisfy you."

"Actually that would not satisfy me." Ike's sense of frustration was increasing, and anger was not far behind. "I am still concerned about your unwillingness to admit that you are using your culture as an excuse to promote religious indoctrination."

The headmaster leaned forward with his elbows on his desk and his hands clasped as if he was praying, "You said this before, but I have answered every one of your complaints. Why do you persist saying that this is indoctrination? There is no such thing going on here. Not a single student has ever come to me to complain about this."

The last statement gave Ike another avenue to pursue. "Don't you know what this is doing to the students? It's becoming a divisive factor that is disrupting the good relations between the Muslim and American kids. Don't you know that there are many American students taking part in religious activities so the Muslim students will accept them? Is that what you want?"

The headmaster leaned back in his chair and spoke softly. "No it is not. And I say to you in all honesty that I have seen no evidence of that."

Exasperated, Ike struggled to say something to make this man understand. "What about the prayers? What about the pressure on the American students who are Christian to participate in the Muslim prayers in school?"

"Mr. Goodman, are you a religious man?"

This was an unexpected question and it startled Ike. Why was he asking such an irrelevant question? Ike responded briskly, "Yes, I would say I'm a religious man."

"Then surely you cannot object to a school allowing freedom of religious expression? You see, it is mandatory for Muslims to pray five times a day, and two of those times occur during the school hours. We would be asking the Muslim students to violate their religious beliefs if we refused to allow them to pray. As for the students who are not Muslims, they can choose to pray or not pray. It is totally up to them."

Here was the basis for an argument that should clearly explain the central issue, and Ike was animated by that hope as he responded. "But when you allow the Muslim students to engage in these prayers in the classroom, it makes it look as if the school is endorsing that one religion, and that implies that all other religions are inferior!" As Ike spoke his voice became louder. When the headmaster responded it was in a calm tone that seemed intentionally exaggerated in order to contrast with the emotion he heard in Ike's voice.

"There is no need to get angry, Mr. Goodman. I am sorry to say this but I am beginning to think that the problem here is really you." Ike was surprised at this response and his face flushed bright red. "Yes, I think that perhaps you are the intolerant person here. Can you tell me why are you so negative toward our Muslim faith?"

Ike felt as if he had the wind knocked out of him. "I've got nothing against your religion!"

"Do you think it is a good religion?"

"Well, to be honest I don't know much about it, but I'm sure it's a religion that advocates good behavior, moral behavior."

"Then if it is a good religion, and you are a religious man, how can exposure to something good be harmful to your son and to the other American students?"

The headmaster's smile reflected his assurance that with this statement their discussion was concluded. As far as he was concerned, there was nothing left to say, but Ike did have something to say, and he would use the headmaster's own words.

"Look, we can both agree that your religion is a good religion, but the problem is that your religion is not my religion. You have students from different religions attending your school, and you are making it difficult for them to accept one another if you do things that seem to favor one religion over another. Most importantly, your Constitution stipulates that in this country people should be free to worship as they please, that the state should not establish one religion as the best or promote one particular religion but keep church and state separate like we do in the United States. That's what I was told and that's what I was assured it would be like here when I made my decision to come here and to send my son to your school. I thought your school would operate just like the public schools do in America."

"But we do, Mr. Goodman. I think we operate our schools just like the schools in America." Brimming with confidence of the truth of his assertion, the headmaster looked at Ike with a most disconcerting smile.

ৰু  ৰু  ৰু

## ECHOES

*One may no more live in the world
without picking up the moral prejudices
of the world than one will be able to
go to Hell without perspiring.*
H. L. Mencken

*Everyone is a prisoner of his own
experiences. No one can eliminate
prejudices—just recognize them.*
Edward R. Murrow

*If you see in any given situation only
what everybody else can see, you can be
said to be so much a representative of
your culture that you are a victim of it.*
S. I. Hayakawa

*When intelligent people behave
stupidly, we are in the presence of
powerful forces.*
William Perry

*No one has ever been born a Negro
hater, a Jew hater, or any other kind of
hater. Nature refuses to be involved in
such suicidal practices.*
Harry Bridges

*We are now at the point where we must
decide whether we are to honor the
concept of a plural society which gains
strength through diversity or whether we
are to have bitter fragmentation that will
result in perpetual tension and strife.*
Earl Warren

*What is the current idea of loyalty? It is
above all, conformity. It is the
unquestioning and uncritical acceptance
of America as it is . . . America as a
finished product, perfect and complete.*
Henry Steele Commager

*America is a passionate idea or it is
nothing. America is a human
brotherhood or it is chaos.*

Max Lerner

*It is a curious fact that of all the illusions
that beset humankind, none is quite so
curious as that tendency to suppose that
we are mentally and morally superior to
those who differ from us in opinion.*

Elbert Hubbard

*We think so because other people all think so,
Or because—or because—after all we do think so,
Or because we were told so, and think we must think so,
Or because we once thought so, and think we still think so,
Or because having thought so, we think we will think so.*

Henry Sidgwick

*Where we all think alike, no one thinks
very much.*

Walter Lippman

*People have one thing in common;
they are all different.*

Robert Zend

*Commandment number one of any truly
civilized society is this: let people be
different.*

David Grayson

*The test of courage comes when we are
in the minority, the test of tolerance
comes when we are in the majority.*

Ralph W. Sockman

*Tolerance is the positive and cordial
effort to understand another's beliefs,
practices, and habits without necessarily
sharing or accepting them.*

Joshua Liebman

*Every society honors its live conformists
and its dead troublemakers.*

Mignon McLaughlin

# LIKE A WHALE

Hamlet: *Do you see yonder cloud that's almost in shape of a camel?*
Polonius: *By the mass and 'tis like a camel indeed.*
Hamlet: *Methinks it is like a weasel.*
Polonius: *It is backed like a weasel.*
Hamlet: *Or like a whale.*
Polonius: *Very like a whale* [3, p. 955].

From childhood we are taught to conform, to agree with others, especially if the other is a person in authority or with status, including those whose status is determined by popularity among their peers. The only people with whom it is safe to disagree are the disagreeable (and powerless) people—the people who do not conform to the group, whether by willful choice or because of a condition over which they have no control.

Despite the nostalgia associated with childhood, an honest remembrance of things past will inevitably include for most people scenes notable for their cruelty, often involving taunts and name calling. The theme for such denigrating language was often based on perceived differences between speaker and victim. Often the difference was a physical anomaly—a birthmark or a scar or a change as mundane as someone suddenly wearing glasses. One visual image from my memories of a rural Midwestern childhood features a group of boys playing together during recess while a plump girl stood nearby watching us. Suddenly one boy began singing the words to a familiar polka melody and was quickly joined by the rest:

> I don't want her.
> You can have her.
> She's too fat for me.

The last line was repeated twice, each repetition sung with increasing volume followed by an enthusiastic encore of the entire performance. The girl's cheeks turned bright red and the color spread throughout her face and down her neck as she turned abruptly and walked away. The boys brayed their triumph with derisive laughter.

Physical differences were not the only cause for contempt, other causes could be much more intellectually sophisticated. The epithet "sissy," though quite common, requires the speaker to comprehend abstract notions of masculinity and femininity and to have a strong sense of normal and abnormal behavior. These abstract concepts provide the basis for making a judgment about particular behaviors as meeting, or failing to meet, the masculine standards. If the behavior does not meet the standards, the violation of gender norms is often severely punished. The greater acceptance of girls called "tomboys" whose behaviors reflect masculine norms more than feminine ones simply demonstrates the degree to which masculine behaviors are the norm for all behavior in a sexist society.

It does not take a prophet to predict the likely outcome from such childhood experiences. Many of these children became adults with rigid notions of gender roles and little tolerance of individual differences. Intolerance is pervasive in our society. There are obvious problems stemming from differences of gender or race, and these problems can be found in our language. Any analysis of English will reveal manifestations of various prejudices embedded in words and expressions, including such common colloquialisms as "I jewed him down," or "You children are acting like a bunch of wild Indians." In addition, the basis for much of our humor is to ridicule the intelligence of members of a particular group determined by such things as race, ethnicity, social class, a disability . . . and gender, of course. If each of us were to review all of the jokes that he or she could remember, and then eliminate those which are demeaning to any group of people, how many jokes would remain?

Intolerance can even exist for differences of opinion. How do people respond to someone who articulates a different perspective on an issue, especially if it is contrary to their own? In my experience people have responded with varying degrees of discomfort. Some seem to ignore the difference and others choose to walk away. A few people respond by arguing briefly, but unless a conciliatory response is made even these few tend to drop the issue or change the subject. In my experience both in and outside of classrooms, it is not often that an individual will oppose the majority on an issue for more than a moment. If someone persists, the result is a growing discomfort followed by frustration and finally anger if the disagreeable person still refuses to accept the majority view.

In discussions where the other person has a conflicting point of view, it is logical that the discussion may have to end by agreeing to disagree, and this should be an acceptable conclusion. Often it is not. After such a discussion, it no longer surprises me when I suddenly begin to receive copies of newspaper articles or magazine essays or research abstracts which offer additional information supporting the other person's point of view.

I attended a speech by a feminist who spoke for an hour in praise of women, but after the speech when she took questions from the audience she was confronted by an angry male who asked, "What have you got against men?" Similar reactions can occur when the issue is more personal. During a panel presentation by students who had just successfully completed student teaching, the panelists were asked to identify professors who had been particularly significant in preparing them for teaching. Each panelist mentioned one or two names. Afterwards a colleague who had not been named by any of the panelists turned to me and said, "What am I, chopped liver?" I was dismayed to hear this. It was important to applaud the professors who had been named and to celebrate such tributes, too seldom given. I did not assume that the absence of my name or that of any of my colleagues was a criticism. I had no doubt that there were other students on our campus who would have mentioned the name of the colleague who felt slighted if they had been on that panel.

These examples illustrate dualistic thinking, sometimes called either/or thinking. This perspective divides everything into two categories: true or false; good or bad; right or wrong. There can be no ambiguity in dualistic thought, and "Truth" is touted as absolute and eternal. Dualism promotes reactions such as "If you say women are good, you must be implying that men are bad." This kind of reaction is a major obstacle preventing people from viewing human differences in a positive way. According to theories of cognitive development, all of us begin life as dualistic thinkers, but as we become more intellectually sophisticated we develop an ability to view the world in more complex ways. Despite this intellectual potential, despite a college education, many people remain dualistic thinkers throughout their adult lives.

Dualistic thinking among adults could explain the reactions of people who become defensive in response to any perceived or genuine challenge to their beliefs. They are not content to think that their beliefs are right for them; they insist with great conviction that their beliefs are universally true and therefore right for everyone. Someone with different beliefs does not merely challenge the dualistic thinker, but is a threat to the rational and moral order of world. In ordinary situations, threats will only provoke a verbal response, but in times of stress or if alcohol has been consumed, a perceived threat may provoke an aggressive physical response.

In the novel *Moby Dick,* Herman Melville describes how small a whale's brain is compared to its body size and by contrast, how much larger is the human brain compared to the average human body size [4]. In describing the sperm whale, Melville notes that its eyes are on each side of its enormous head which would be analogous to human beings having eyes where their ears are. This evolutionary development requires the sperm whale to coordinate in that relatively tiny brain two completely different views of its world, two different perspectives. With our comparatively larger and more sophisticated brains, Melville wonders why it should be so difficult for human beings to do the same.

It is a fair question, and the survival of our species may well depend on our ability to hold more than one perspective in our minds at one time, just like the sperm whale. This must go beyond simply being aware of other points of view because most people already have such an awareness. To see the world from more than one perspective, however, requires a person to understand the different perspectives and why each one represents a feasible way of looking at and living in the world. Only then will we be able to accept and affirm diversity.

Being able to understand those who are different is a worthwhile goal in any society. It is especially necessary in a society as diverse as the United States, yet many Americans persist in perceiving differences as divisive. Although people are increasingly inclined to express public pieties about the value of diversity, their words are often not reflected in their deeds. Instead their actions suggest not only that they do not value or appreciate diversity, but that they do not even tolerate differences. This intolerance is illustrated in the mixed messages stemming from the use of the phrase "color blind."

When Civil Rights leaders like Martin Luther King, Jr. and Thurgood Marshall advocated a color blind society, they were talking about equality before the law and providing an equal opportunity for Americans of all colors. They used the phrase in the context of widespread institutional discrimination that prevented the United States from achieving the desired goal of rewarding individuals based on merit and not on race. When past Presidents like Ronald Reagan and Lyndon Johnson referred to a color blind society, they were usually not referring to the issue of institutional discrimination but to individual perceptions. Many people of color have interpreted such comments to mean that the way to solve racial problems is to ignore the color of someone's skin. Does this mean white people must pretend that people of color have no color, that they are white, in order for white people to view them in a positive way? Is ignoring a person's skin color the only way to have harmony in a diverse society?

In the United States we have a history of segregating those who are different in some way from the majority. It is a history that we are still trying to overcome. Although we struggle with the issue, the depth of our difficulty with differences is even more obvious when it involves less volatile issues than race or religion or sexual orientation. When people talk about a recent movie they have seen or a novel they have read, the question "How did you like it?" is often met with this response, "It was *different.*" Different in this context typically means unusual or even strange and it often means bad. "It was different" becomes code language for "I didn't like it." Anyone hearing such comments understands that the speaker did not perceive the film or book to have merit and is not recommending it.

What a paradox. We live in a society of incredible diversity, yet most people do not value that diversity. We have avoided those who were different through segregated neighborhoods and segregated schools. We have also tried to reduce differences to create a greater degree of trust and acceptance between different groups. This has been illustrated in our historic responses to immigration and in our government's immigration policies.

In response to the steady flow of immigrants into the United States at the end of the nineteenth century, public schools were assigned the responsibility of Americanizing immigrant children and youth. The outcome of the Americanization effort was that several generations of students were taught to discard their ethnic traditions, reject their heritage, forget whatever language was spoken in their home, and accept a narrowly defined image of an American as the ideal toward which they should strive. Americanization meant that the children of immigrants learned to be ashamed of their parents for clinging to the "old ways." White ethnic groups who immigrated to the United States were relatively successful under such a system, but immigrants who were not white were not as well received nor rewarded. Differences in skin color remained an obstacle in the pursuit of happiness, in the quest to achieve the American Dream [5].

This Americanization effort was embraced so enthusiastically it was even extended to the boarding schools operated by the Bureau of Indian Affairs. In these schools Indian children were educated like white children so that they would become like white children. The schools were usually located far from the reservation so that it was not possible for the children to go home and visit their parents. Officials were afraid that such visits would result in the children going "back to the blanket," meaning they would return to Indian ways. Few Americans at that time perceived the irony of this goal: to Americanize the indigenous inhabitants of America.

Today many people claim that this is all behind us, that America has progressed in a positive direction toward an acceptance of diversity. Our diverse ethnic heritage was celebrated during the televised festivities in 1990 which commemorated the restoration of Ellis Island. Corporate consultants such as John Naisbitt have promoted the value of diversity, and recent developments suggest that corporate America respects diversity and recognizes that it's in their best interest to do so. One might believe that we are entering an age of enlightenment with a public consensus regarding the value of the incredible diversity within American society.

Various incidents and several studies smudge the rose-colored lens. Diversity continues as a source of conflict in America. It is true that our society is promoting pluralistic attitudes more than before; it is also true that we have not reached a consensus about valuing our differences.

This dilemma is illustrated in the experience of a student teacher who had been assigned to a third grade classroom at a Midwestern school with predominantly white students and a white female teacher. As the month of February approached, the supervising teacher suggested that the student teacher create a new bulletin board for the month. Wanting to be creative rather than using the conventional hearts and flowers associated with Valentine's Day, the student teacher developed ideas for celebrating February as Black History month. She paged through professional journals for appropriate pictures and collected quotations by important African Americans. She searched for other images for what she imagined as a display that would be both attractive and educational.

When she discussed her idea with the supervising teacher, the student teacher was initially enthusiastic, but began to falter as she sensed a lack of support in her listener. After the student teacher had described her proposed bulletin board, the supervising teacher politely but firmly rejected the proposal. Realizing the student teacher's disappointment, the supervising teacher explained why this proposal would be inappropriate for third grade students, "They're a little too young for that." The explanation only confused the student teacher even more. What was it that these white third graders were too young to be exposed to—African Americans?

Many colleges and universities require students to take courses dealing with diversity. No matter what profession they choose, college students today will encounter diversity throughout their lives. Such courses are offered as an attempt to prepare them for that diversity, but how are these young people supposed to accept and respect diversity if they have previously been taught to be suspicious and distrustful of differences? If the experiences these students have had in school before coming to college has been based on the traditional curriculum rather than on multicultural perspectives, how effective can one or two college courses be?

If students come to college without having read essays, stories, and poetry written by authors from diverse groups, if they have not studied history from the perspectives of Native Americans or Africans brought here as slaves, on what basis do they build an understanding of diversity? If they have not been acquainted with the struggles of the working class nor of women, if their bulletin boards and textbook illustrations portrayed people primarily as white and male, on what basis can they create images of America and Americans that reflect the actual diversity of our society? How can young people manage in only four years to unlearn all the myths and stereotypes and misinformation they have learned during the previous eighteen years?

A major obstacle in promoting respect for diversity is the perception of many white people that the only beneficiaries of this change will be people of color or women or other oppressed groups. If our society is to value diversity, it is essential that we all make one fundamental assumption: everyone who lives in a society as diverse as the United States will benefit if we genuinely value diversity rather than merely pretend to do so. If we ignore our differences they will not disappear. Demographers have been unequivocal, and frankly conservative, in their predictions that diversity in America will not only continue but increase. Our response to this diversity will shape our future as a nation.

The future could include increased cooperation among diverse groups not only in the United States but globally as well. This global cooperation will become increasingly necessary if we are to improve economic opportunities, address environmental challenges, solve political disputes, and enjoy the results of cross-cultural influences in literature, music, and art. The future could also present us with increasing isolationism and inter-ethnic conflicts. If such ethnic fragmentation occurs, it will not be because we tried to accept and respect diversity as some critics contend, it will be the consequence of one powerful group or nation imposing itself on others. Such attempts always produce aggressive responses by members of oppressed groups in an effort to affirm their cultural and individual identity while rejecting, often violently, the impositions of the dominant group. Dominant group persistence will produce separatist sentiments pitting one group against another, one nation against another. Efforts to reduce differences in the interest of greater harmony are likely to be met with suspicion, if not hostility. The best outcome one could hope for in such a world would be to promote simple tolerance among people. Surely we can do better.

To do better will not be easy. We should begin by recognizing that this is not about choosing between liberalism and conservatism. It is about improving our schools and our neighborhoods; it is about dramatic changes affecting how and where we work. We are a diverse society. If we are to be a good society for all people, as individuals we must become more knowledgeable about the diverse groups within our society.

Educating people to value diversity is the first step to a better future, and that is the task for our schools. A Chinese proverb says, "if you are thinking one year ahead, sow a seed. If you are thinking ten years ahead, plant a tree. If you are thinking a hundred years ahead, educate the people." Education that effectively promotes respect for diversity is required to realize our potential as a diverse society. Education that promotes the idea of accepting diversity while still demanding conformity to one perspective is a sham, and hypocrisy has never been effective as a pedagogical strategy.

Educators cannot guarantee a better society because what happens in schools is only part of what is necessary to achieve that goal, but education can provide the basis for a good society. An education that includes diverse perspectives and values alternative explanations will promote the development of a society that views itself as favored rather than fragmented by diversity. Various community organizations, from businesses to churches to the Boy Scouts, can contribute to this goal, but schools are essential. Teachers must help students learn new ways of looking at their world and challenge them to comprehend contradictory ideas and conflicting perspectives. This kind of education will be essential if young people are to function effectively in a complex world. To be successful in a diverse society and in the global economy, people must learn to view the world like a whale.

# CHAPTER FIVE
## In the Key of E: EMPATHY

### SHARING THE PAIN

George Gordon (Lord Byron) and Robert Peel were schoolmates at Harrow. One day Byron saw Peel being given a vicious beating with a belt wielded by a much older, larger boy. He could see that Peel was frightened and in great pain. Byron could not physically prevent the bigger boy from beating his friend because of his small size and his clubfoot, but when he approached them Byron grabbed the boy's right arm to prevent the next blow and asked how many stripes he intended to inflict upon his friend. "What's that to you?" growled the bully.

Byron managed to hide his feelings of helplessness and rage. "Because, if you please," he replied calmly, "I would take half" [1, p. 44].

> **Empathy**—intellectual identification with the feelings, thoughts or attitudes of another person . . . the capacity for participation in (or vicarious experiencing of) another's feelings or ideas.

Not only do many people confuse empathy with sympathy, so do some lexicographers. In several dictionaries sympathy is listed as a synonym for empathy, despite the differences between the two. Empathy is the ability to relate intimately to someone in their situation, whether the other is joyful or sorrowful, enthusiastic or enraged. To sympathize is to share a feeling, but to empathize is to have a profound awareness of the emotional state of another.

Empathy is not just about emotions but includes an intellectual aspect which provides the clearest distinction from sympathy. Sympathy is generic but empathy is specific. Empathy requires that you understand how a particular person feels. This understanding is based on knowledge of another so intimate that it permits you to know what that person is feeling. Based on this cognitive understanding, a person is able to engage their own emotions to replicate the feelings of the other person. Although anyone would suffer from a beating, Byron was

97

cognizant of Peel's sensitive nature and had a deeper understanding of the immense suffering such a beating would cause his friend. He was not big enough to overcome Peel's tormentor by force, but he felt the boy's pain so intensely that it was as if he were being beaten as well. From such a profound sense of empathy, it was possible for Byron to do the only thing he could do to alleviate his friend's suffering: offer to take some of the blows himself.

In situations where comforting words are called for, people say, "I know how you feel." This response may be rejected if the recipient believes that sympathy rather than empathy is being expressed. Sometimes the rejection can be angry: "No you don't! You can't possibly know how I feel!" Such a response may be perceived as rude, or at least an indication of the person's emotional turmoil. In reality the statement is more likely to be a reaction against what is perceived as a diminishment or even a trivialization of the person's agonizing and possibly traumatizing experience.

> **Sympathy**—having common feelings, being able to share in a feeling or feelings, a harmony of agreement in feeling . . . an impulse of compassion. . . the feeling brought about by such sensitivity (e.g., "Having sympathy for the poor").

To claim to know how someone feels suggests empathy, a claim of intimate knowledge of the other. Sympathy is simply an expression of emotion. To be sympathetic is to be touched by an experience, either a fictional or an actual one, and saying:

(I can imagine how I would feel if I were in this situation . . .)
*I know how you feel.*

but to express empathy is to say:

(I can imagine you in this situation and I know how it would affect you . . .)
*I know how you feel.*

Sympathy does not go as deep as empathy. It is not about understanding but is simply about feeling, about having an *impulse of compassion.* Although sympathy is based on sensitivity, it is not always and not necessarily sensitivity to the feelings of the other. Feeling sympathy does not require a person to understand another, only that a person knows how he or she would feel in a situation similar to what the other person is experiencing. One can have *sympathy for the poor* and not understand the destructive force of poverty and the daily struggle required to survive poverty. One can have *sympathy for the poor* and still denounce welfare recipients.

It is not difficult to feel sympathy. Most people find it easy to respond sympathetically to someone's troubles, but sometimes sympathy is inadequate. Some situations require more than being touched by emotion; they require people to take the time to understand another. This can be especially important if the other is someone different, especially if they are from a group that has been stigmatized. People must learn to go beyond sympathy and develop empathy.

This is not to suggest that people should feel empathy all of the time for every human being in any situation, but it is possible to feel and express empathy at appropriate times. There are times when simply expressing sympathy is enough. When my nineteen-year-old son was killed in a car accident, I was grateful for the many expressions of sympathy. People who did not know me intimately would say how horrible they would feel if they lost one of their children. I appreciated what they were saying. This is a common fear for parents. I was surprised, however, when one very close friend said, "I can't imagine what it would be like to lose my child. I can't imagine how that would feel." Although I heard the sincere sound of consolation in his voice, I was confused by what he said. He knew me well enough to imagine the pain I was feeling, but he said he couldn't imagine it.

As I thought about his comments, I realized that in contrast to the sympathy expressed by others, he had gone further. His comments represented a complex expression of empathy. He could understand the pain of the loss inflicted upon me, and he did not want to feel it. I had no choice but to bear the burden of my son's death, but he could choose to imagine how this had hurt me or not. By refusing even to imagine it, he was saying in a profoundly compassionate way how deeply he understood the sorrow I was forced to endure. His heartfelt empathy sustains me still as I continue wrestling with the angel of grief, asking not for a blessing but for a lessening of the pain. That would be blessing enough for me.

### è&   è&   è&
## HEARING VOICES

*If anyone says, "I love God," and hates*
*his brother, he is a liar, for he who does*
*not love his brother whom he has seen,*
*cannot love God whom he has not seen.*

John 1 (4:20)

*But evil is wrought by want of thought,*
*As well as want of heart!*
                          Thomas Hood

> *Nothing begins and nothing ends*
> *That is not paid with moan;*
> *For we are born in other's pain,*
> *And perish in our own.*
>                       Francis Thompson

*God could not be everywhere and*
*therefore he made mothers.*
                          Jewish Proverb

> *To correct the evils, great and small,*
> *which spring from want of sympathy*
> *and from enmity among strangers, as*
> *nations or as individuals, is one of*
> *the highest functions of civilization.*
>                       Abraham Lincoln

*We have too many high sounding words,*
*and too few actions that correspond*
*with them.*
                          Abigail Adams

> *I pity the poor in bondage that have none*
> *to help them. That is why I am here (on*
> *trial for the Harper's Ferry incident) . . .*
> *It is (because of) my sympathy with the*
> *oppressed and wronged who are as good*
> *as you and as precious in the sight of*
> *God . . . Had I interfered on behalf of*
> *the rich, the powerful . . . the so-called*
> *great, every man in this courtroom*
> *would have deemed it an act worthy*
> *of reward rather than punishment.*
>                       John Brown

*We are all strong enough to bear the*
*misfortunes of others.*
                 Duc de La Rochefoucauld

> *We are just statistics, born to*
> *consume resources.*
>                             Horace

*If all our misfortunes were laid in one
common heap whence everyone must take
an equal portion, most people would be
contented to take their own and depart.*
                                    Socrates

*What plays mischief with the truth is
that men will insist upon the universal
application of a temporary feeling or
opinion.*
                            Herman Melville

*Fraud and falsehood only dread
examination. Truth invites it.*
                        Thomas Cooper

*There is no greater lie than a truth
misunderstood.*
                            William James

*The truth is rarely pure, and never
simple.*
                        Oscar Wilde

*It takes two to speak the truth—one to
speak and another to hear.*
                        Henry David Thoreau

*Misunderstandings and inertia cause
perhaps more to go wrong in this world
than slyness and evil intent.*
            Johann Wolfgang von Goethe

*There is so much good in the worst of us,
And so much bad in the best of us,
That it hardly becomes any of us
To talk about the rest of us.*
                                Anonymous

*Praise is the best diet for us, after all.*
                    Rev. Sydney Smith

*I have striven not to laugh at human
actions, not to weep at them, nor to
hate them, but to understand them.*
                            Baruch Spinoza

## VARIATIONS ON A THEME

During the 1950s I attended a one-room school from Kindergarten through seventh grade. My rural school district was so small that during my fourth-, fifth-, and sixth-grade years I was the only child in my grade. I was not happy about this, but I had no choice. Not having a choice was a common occurrence at my school, and at all the other rural schools. We had gloves and bats and balls to play softball, but the only way we had enough players to put two teams on the field was to let almost everyone play—girls and boys, younger and older. These were usually high scoring games because the younger children would play in the outfield and they were as likely to run away from the ball as try to catch it. Any batter who got the ball out of the infield could always count on extra bases, and a simple line drive would become a home run. The only way to have an exciting, competitive game was to invite a team from another rural school to play against us. By selecting our best nine players, we could put a fairly good team on the field and so could the other side. The nine best players always included girls.

Although we only used one classroom in my school, the building had housed a high school in the 1930s. There was a baseball diamond in the large field next to the school and sand pits for long jump and high jump; therefore, my school always hosted the track and field competitions for students from all the other rural schools in our area. Levels of competition were not determined by age or grade level or gender but by a far more appropriate criterion: weight. All children weighing ninety to ninety-nine pounds competed against each other as did all children weighing eighty to eighty-nine pounds and so on. This ensured that children who were maturing rapidly did not engage in unfair competition with their age peers, but had to compete against others whose physical development was similar.

Determining competitors by weight meant that boys and girls competed against each other for the blue, red, yellow, and white ribbons signifying first, second, third, and fourth place finishes respectively. In my seventh-grade year I remember watching and cheering as my schoolmate Patty Jensen out-raced a crowded field in the 100 yard dash. I was not so cheerful eating Linda Blair's dust, literally, on the gravel road in front of the school. Although she was the only girl in the race, Linda showed the boys her heels in the 100 yard dash. I was next to last out of nine sprinters, but I could not complain. Linda was my first classmate after three solitary years, so I was glad she was there and I was also a little in love with her. Unfortunately, I confessed my love in bad poetry which caused her considerable embarrassment.

The games we played were not always equitable; many of them taught sexist attitudes so common in our culture. Boys played basketball while girls played hopscotch; boys played football while girls played word games. But those activities are not as vivid for me as the games that boys and girls played together: pom pom pullaway; red rover; hide and seek; kick the can; annie-i-over; may I; red light/green light. The older boys and girls were supposed to look out for the younger children. Boys and girls played together as friends; gender didn't matter much. What mattered was having fun.

As my elementary school years were ending, one-room schools were disappearing in rural Nebraska. In my village we preserved the school for a few more years by joining with a school district in the neighboring town. Students in kindergarten through sixth grade stayed in our village school but the five of us in seventh and eighth grades boarded the yellow school bus for the five-mile ride. Instead of one classmate for my eighth grade year, I now had more than thirty! I was excited about that, and nervous, too. This was junior high. We were beginning to be interested in the opposite sex. Notes were passed when teachers were not looking and intense, hurried conversations happened between classes. There was another important difference about being in junior high—all of the activities were now segregated. Boys and girls did not compete against each other and we were together only for school dances and social events.

Like most of the boys, I competed in football, basketball, and track. Some girls competed for the honor of being a cheerleader, the rest joined the Pep Club to support the boys. This was before federal laws compelled schools to offer comparable athletic activities for girls. At the time I didn't think much about it, but now I wonder how Linda Blair or Patty Jensen felt about not having the chance to compete. Did they wonder why their athletic abilities were no longer needed? What did they do with all those blue ribbons?

In high school the gender roles hardened because of the prominence of sports in school life. Boys were central, girls were peripheral. One of the greatest achievements for a girl was to date an athlete, especially if he was part of the starting lineup for the football or basketball teams, or if he was a winner in track and field competitions. By the time we were seniors, the boys in my class had learned their gender lessons well: it was better to be a boy than a girl. We didn't talk about it, but we all knew it.

I still remember going to dances and watching some of the most attractive girls refusing to dance whenever a boy would ask them. These were the popular girls who dated the best athletes. They danced with each other all evening, waiting patiently and faithfully for their boyfriends to arrive. It was common for many of the athletes to go out drinking beer before coming to the dance. They would typically show up for the final fifteen to twenty minutes when they didn't have to pay admission. They danced with their girlfriends until the dance was over. Their demeanor was arrogant, even a bit contemptuous. I didn't like their behavior, but I was also puzzled about why the girls allowed their boyfriends to treat them in such a cavalier manner.

Part of my confusion was based on my experiences. I grew up with sisters and had female friends, even in high school. Conversations with girls covered current events, politics, books, movies, relationships, rumors, and all sorts of interesting issues. Conversations with boys tended to focus on cars, sex, and sports. I had no interest in the first topic and little knowledge of the second, so I was limited to talking about sports. Much of the talk about sex sounded like sheer bravado or else it degenerated into crude jokes. I didn't like the jokes, and I didn't like all the masculine posturing. I especially hated the locker room.

I remember the sting of a towel snapped on bare buttocks. It was not fun. I remember the friend punching me in the shoulder and knowing I had to punch him back. If I did not I would be confronted with the worst accusation you can make to a boy—"What are you, a sissy?" So I punched my friend in the shoulder, hard, and we exchanged several more shoulder punches. I remember thinking how stupid it seemed, and I remember how my shoulder ached afterwards.

When I went to college in the late 1960s, there was as much happening outside the classroom as inside. Men rejected traditional masculine images and sported long hair and beards and earrings. Women also rebelled against the traditional feminine images, jeans replaced dresses and they questioned sex-role stereotypes. Men and women participated in Vietnam War protests and listened sympathetically to the call for Black Power and Chicano Power. The voices of minorities were denouncing prejudice and demanding change, and women were also finding their voice. Everything was being challenged.

Women on my campus objected to the curfew for women in residence halls because there was no curfew for men. Heated discussions with campus administrators lead to the compromise of issuing keys for the residence hall doors to women who were seniors so they could return to the hall past the curfew hour when the doors were locked. This compromise was inadequate and would not last. Before long colleges were experimenting with coeducational residence halls.

Women demanded more funding for women's sports after Title IX became the law of the land. Feminists were publishing provocative essays and books, opening a window on a brave new world. These women asked different questions, gave different answers. They made me examine my assumptions about men and women. They helped me to see old issues in new ways, as did the writers of color and the war protestors and the reformers.

When I became a high school teacher I tried to bring this kind of intellectual excitement to my students. Although they responded well to most issues, the students did not want to discuss gender issues. It was too personal, too threatening. One of the main goals for an adolescent is to be popular with the opposite sex, and neither male nor female wanted to jeopardize that. When I began teaching in college I discovered this was true for these students as well.

During a discussion in one of my college classes, I argued that men could benefit by rejecting some of the qualities traditionally associated with masculinity. A young man who was majoring in elementary education spoke to me after class. He did not disagree with me, but he said men paid a price for rejecting the masculine role. He wanted to teach in an elementary school because he was a gentle, nurturing person, so he had chosen a profession which valued those qualities. He was happy with his choice, but the women he met did not respond positively to those attributes in a man. They were more attracted to men exhibiting conventional masculine qualities. I suggested that this might only be true in his experience, but he had talked to other men who said it was true for them as well. He believed men would not change if women were not attracted to men who abandoned the masculine stereotype.

I had to agree that women influence male behavior. Although men should be responsible for themselves, most people change only if it is in their self-interest. Since adolescents, and young adults in particular, have a compelling self-interest in being perceived as attractive, young men would be more likely to reject the gender stereotypes if traditional masculine behavior was no longer attractive to young women. If those gender roles are going to change, the driving force for this revolution is not likely to be young men but older men who have established successful relationships and have the self-confidence to challenge the status quo.

Social observers have argued that men are changing, but in a different direction. Men have become more violent toward women, especially in their use of sexual violence. For years date rape was the crime that had no name. Although not a new phenomenon, date rape seems to be more common today. Some feminists claim it stems from the increasing pressure on men to prove their masculinity. A real man is ruthless; a real man doesn't take no for an answer; a real man "scores" with every woman he dates. It's hard to live down to these standards without resorting to force, or something else.

At a Freshman orientation, a college counselor was discussing date rape with a group of young men and his message was simple: if a woman says no, she means no; if you force her to have sex after she says no, that is a rape and rape is a crime. The counselor concluded the session by asking if anyone had questions. A young man raised his hand—a blond, blue eyed son of rural, white America. Their dialogue was brief but revealing:

"What if she doesn't say anything?"

"What do you mean?"

"Well," the young man paused, then glanced at the other men and smiled, "what if she can't say anything because she's drunk and passed out? That's not rape is it?"

Although the situation described by this young man would be considered rape, alcohol remains the weapon of choice in the battleground of the sexes. A new option is to use rohypnatol, a drug better known as "roofies," which not only renders a woman physically immobile but disrupts her mental processes so she is unable to recall what happened while she was helpless. This has become known as the date rape drug. The desire to have sexual intercourse with an unconscious and unresponsive partner is a chilling illustration of the extent to which some men are willing to go to achieve an illusion of masculine power. Power is the primary gratification men seek from rape, but raping a comatose women seems more like an act of necrophilia than an act of sexual conquest.

Although there is agreement that such examples are not isolated phenomena, some social analysts claim that statistics on rape and sexual assault have been inflated. The debate over the accuracy of the quantitative data is likely to continue, but there are also qualitative measures. When discussing sexual violence with women who know and trust me, they have described their own experiences with rape or sexual assault. Based on what they have told me, it seems realistic to assume that almost every woman has experienced some form of sexual violence.

Toward the end of one fall semester, a young woman stopped coming to my class. She was a vibrant, articulate physical education major looking forward to graduation in the spring. It didn't make sense that she would stop coming to class without an explanation. If she didn't pass my class she wouldn't be able to graduate. When I tried to call her she wasn't available, so I left a message that she should see me right away. She came during my office hours the next day, but she did not exude confidence as before. She was upset, shaky. She apologized for missing class; she had some personal problems she was trying to resolve. I offered to help. I did not want her to receive a low grade because she had been doing so well up to this point. Slowly, hesitantly, she told me what had happened.

Her father had a friend whose truck route came through campus and ended in her hometown. Her father had suggested that she ask the driver for a ride whenever she wanted to come home. She only had to call the man and tell him where he could find her Friday afternoon and she could ride home with him. He could also take her back on Monday since he would get to campus before her first class. She had been going home with him since the previous school year. The driver was married and had two children. She enjoyed talking with him and they often joked and teased each other. He was a nice guy.

She rode home with him the day before Thanksgiving. Shortly after picking her up he stopped at a bar and said he would buy her a drink. They had a few beers and talked. Back in the truck he seemed quieter than usual. After driving in silence for several miles, he pulled the truck off the road and parked. She asked him what he was doing, but he just grabbed her and started kissing her. She tried to fight him off but he was too aggressive. He gripped her wrist tightly as he crawled into the sleeping compartment behind the cab and then pulled her in after him, pulling on her hair with his other hand to make sure she didn't resist. Once in the compartment he continued to grope and grab. The young woman paused at this point in her story. She had been looking at the floor, but now she looked at me: "You know, because of my success in athletics I have always looked at myself as a strong person. I always thought I could take care of myself, but I was beginning to realize that I couldn't stop him. He was going to rape me and there was nothing I could do." She shuddered after she said this.

He had unzipped her jeans and had pushed them down when she blurted out: "You can go ahead and do this but don't think for a minute that I'm going to enjoy it." He stopped what he was doing and stared at her, looking puzzled and annoyed. He turned her onto her stomach and spanked her with several stinging slaps. After that he crawled back behind the wheel and drove off. She put her clothes on and stayed in the sleeping compartment until they reached her hometown. She said nothing to him, even when she got out of the truck. She did not tell her father what his friend had done, but she insisted that her father drive her back to campus on Sunday rather than riding back in the truck.

Since she had returned to campus the man had called and left messages about wanting to see her. He did not call to apologize but to pursue their "relationship." The young woman had avoided him so far, but she wasn't sure what she should do. She was still stunned by what had happened. She kept saying, "How could he do that? He's got a wife. He's got two kids. He and my father are friends." I had no answers for her questions, but I am certain that what she said to him saved her from being raped. The man probably pictured himself as an experienced lover seducing a reluctant virgin. By telling him he was forcing her to do something she would not enjoy, she shattered that fantasy. That was why he spanked her. She had spoiled his fun.

I advised her to call him and tell him to stop bothering her or she would tell his wife and her father what he had done. I assured her that this threat would probably stop his calls and she could concentrate on her academic work. By the end of our conversation she seemed to feel better. A few weeks later she stopped by my office during final exam week to thank me for my help. By the time she graduated she seemed to have regained her sense of confidence.

Some feminists believe we have sexualized violence to such a degree in our culture that it has become normalized and it is simply realistic for a woman to expect a certain amount of coercion from a man [2]. At a rape trial the victim will be asked if she said "no." If she did, the next question will be: "How many times did you say "no." The second question implies that saying "no" only one time is not enough, that only a series of rejections will prove that the victim did not send the poor man any "mixed messages" in refusing his amorous advances.

Another common question for the rape victim is: "Did you resist?" Hearing that she did, the next question will be: "How strenuously did you resist?" The second question implies that women should expect to be manhandled. If she doesn't want to have sex, she must say it several times and vigorously resist aggressive advances. Anything less will be regarded as evidence that she really wanted to have sex, so if sex occurs it is not rape. This is called a date.

After a discussion of date rape in a graduate class, one of the students came to my office. She said she wished someone had explained this issue to her when she was younger. When she was an undergraduate she met someone at a party and they started dating. One night after dinner they returned to her apartment for an after dinner drink. They were sitting on the couch when he began to kiss her. He pressed her down on the couch and became very aggressive. While lying on her left arm he grabbed her right wrist with his right hand and began taking off her clothes with his left hand while still kissing her. She begged him to stop but he ignored her. She tried to get free of him but she couldn't. He raped her. She didn't realize it was rape at the time. She didn't know what to call it.

He was walking around the room while she lay on the couch trying to understand what had just happened. She tried to remember if she had said anything to mislead him into thinking she wanted to have sex. She was blaming herself for possibly giving him the wrong impression. He was walking toward the front door when he turned to look at her. "You know you wanted it," he said. He turned back to the door, opened it and left.

At that moment she experienced emotional fireworks as feelings of rage ripped through her. After she calmed down she was clear about one thing: she had not wanted to have sex! She was not certain about much but she was certain about that. What happened was a consequence of his choice not her desire. Later she read about sexual violence and the myths about rape. Although rape is commonly thought of as violence perpetrated by a stranger in a dark alley, in reality most rape victims know their rapist and most rapes occur in a safe place like the victim's home. When it happens on a date it is called date rape. What happened to her had a name.

Date rape is better known today, and many college campuses are implementing preventative measures. Unfortunately this often takes the form of better lighting for pedestrian paths and escort services for women walking late at night. In addition to offering protective services for women, universities ought to be confronting male students. Men and women should be talking about sexuality and relationships, about power and rape. Men should be challenged to answer the questions: Why do some men rape? What can all men do to prevent rape? These questions could be the basis for some critical conversations between men and with women.

These conversations could begin in high school. During a discussion of a love poem some of the senior boys were making comments implying that when it comes to love and sex, girls were either "good girls" or "sluts." The teacher presented the following scenario:

> Imagine that there are two students at our high school—Sam and Sally—who start dating during their senior year. The relationship becomes intense and they start having sex. After a while the relationship starts to deteriorate. Finally they have a huge quarrel and they break up. Here is the question. If any of you guys asked Sally to go on a date and she accepted, how many of you would expect her to have sex with you on that date?

All the boys in the classroom raised their hands. The girls seemed stunned. The teacher asked the boys why they would expect Sally to have sex with them. Their responses included: "She's not a virgin anymore so what's the big deal?" and "What's Sam got that I haven't got?" The girls could no longer contain themselves and they challenged these comments. For perhaps the first time in their lives these young people had a frank discussion with one another about their attitudes toward love and sex and relationships.

In discussing sexism, someone is sure to mention how women are used as sex objects. Men often feel defensive about this. Once I admitted that I enjoyed looking at attractive women and the men challenged me, "What about this business of being a sex object? Weren't you saying we shouldn't do that? Isn't that being sexist?" I said it wasn't necessarily sexist to appreciate physical beauty in anyone, male or female, but it is sexist if that becomes the focus. As an illustration, I told them of a conversation I had with a buxom woman who told me that what irritated her the most was to talk to a man whose eyes never got above her chest. Her comment was an example of how attention to physical attributes can become inappropriate. If a woman is reduced to being only a part of her body, that perception diminishes her as a human being. Such perceptions make date rape more likely.

Men and women have much to offer each other besides sex. In the best marriages, partners are more likely to talk about the quality of their relationship rather than the quality or quantity of their sexual activity. In the best relationships, each person says the other is his or her best friend. In the best friendships, each person will achieve some degree of intimacy with the other, and to achieve intimacy requires empathy. Men will not develop empathy for all women unless they can achieve some degree of intimacy with particular women. Men need to understand how our culture places a priority on masculinity and dismisses femininity. Men must recognize and reject a multitude of messages teaching them to be condescending to women.

Men and women have much to gain by discarding the fossilized definitions of masculine and feminine and redefining themselves as individuals, not as the latest version of ancient gender themes. Men and women have much to gain by disputing the culture's obsession with youth and beauty and reclaiming the virtues of maturity, the value of knowledge and experience, the possibility of wisdom. Men and women have much to gain by rejecting the adolescent sexual fantasies promoted in the media and recognizing the reality of our need for relationship which is as constant as the beating of the human heart. Men and women have much to gain by seeing each other as individuals, as a variation on a human theme. Each person has a chance to contribute something to this evolving melody. If men and women will look at themselves as individuals, each can become part of this unique creation, contributing a note, a word, a verse that the world has never heard before and will never hear again.

## ECHOES

*And while I don't expect you to save the
world, I do think it's not asking too much
for you to love those with whom you
sleep, share the happiness of those whom
you call friend, encourage those among
you who are visionary, and remove from
your life those who offer you despair,
depression and disrespect.*

Nikki Giovanni

*If we suddenly discovered that we had
only five minutes left to say all we wanted
so say, every telephone booth would be
occupied by people trying to call up other
people to stammer that they loved them.*

Christopher Morley

*Washing one's hands of the conflict
between the powerful and the powerless
means to side with the powerful, not to be
neutral.*

Paolo Freire

*In every child who is born, under no
matter what circumstances, and of no
matter what parents, the potentiality
of the human race is born again, and
in him, and in each of us, is a terrific
responsibility towards human life.*

James Agee

*The old know what they want; the young
are sad and bewildered.*

Logan Pearsall Smith

*Experience is not what happens to you; it
is what you do with what happens to you.*

Aldous Huxley

*Think like an active person, act like a
thoughtful person.*

Henri Bergson

*We make more enemies by what we*
*say than friends by what we do.*
John C. Collins

*People ask for criticism, but they only*
*want praise.*
Somerset Maugham

*. . . Human kind*
*Cannot bear very much reality.*
T. S. Eliot

*Thou shalt not sit*
*With statistics nor commit*
*A social science.*
W. H. Auden

*To understand God's thoughts we must*
*study statistics, for these are the*
*measure of his purpose.*
Florence Nightingale

*I have no objection to churches so long*
*as they do not interfere with God's work.*
Brooks Atkinson

*As scarce as truth is, the supply seems*
*greater than the demand.*
Adlai Stevenson

*Most of the people I meet in America are*
*compassionate. Why is it that individually*
*we can be so compassionate and*
*collectively we can be so harsh. . . .*
*I don't have an answer to that.*
Jonathan Kozol

## THE PERVERSION OF HOMOPHOBIA

The young woman was awakened at 3:00 in the morning by the sound of the phone ringing. Struggling to wake up, she fumbled for the phone. She couldn't comprehend at first the torrent of words spewing at her, but it was a woman's agitated voice. Eventually she understood that the caller had cancer and claimed that "I have this cancer because of you!" After a few minutes the caller hung up, leaving the young woman to wonder who the caller was and why she was calling.

At 3:00 the next morning, the phone rang again. The same caller made the same hostile accusation. The young woman interrupted to ask, "Who is this?" but to no avail. The caller ranted for several minutes about the young woman causing her cancer and then hung up. The calls continued to come, night after night, at exactly 3:00. Such calls would upset anyone, but this young woman was a lesbian and she was worried that the caller might become violent, might use this allegation about her being the cause of the cancer as an excuse to stalk her and harm her. The young woman became increasingly distraught.

She and her partner discussed the bizarre situation, but they didn't know what to do. She didn't want to call the police. What was especially frustrating was that the voice sounded vaguely familiar, but she could not quite identify it nor could she think of anyone who would make up such a story to harass her. She couldn't call her family. They were fundamentalist Christians who had ostracized her years ago when she came out of the closet. Her mother refused to see her and the two had not talked since. She was no longer welcome in her parent's home.

After receiving the calls for several weeks, the young woman began to recognize the voice. Listening intently, she said nothing for several more nights until she felt certain she knew the identity of her tormentor. She did not want to believe her suspicions, but she was determined to have a confrontation. When the next call came she only listened for a minute, then interrupted, "Mother, why are you doing this? Why are you saying this to me?" Her mother responded, "God is punishing me because you're a lesbian! I have cancer because of you!" [3].

This story comes not from a soap opera script but from a reality scripted by homophobia. Because of her religious beliefs, the mother had denounced her daughter's homosexuality as a perversion and an abomination. Her child was living in sin and bound for eternal condemnation. When she learned she had cancer she was convinced it was divine punishment for having given birth to such a sinful daughter. In her anger, the mother lashed out at the wilfull child who had "chosen" such a perverse lifestyle and rejected all that was good in the world, including her mother. And the mother's fury was boundless.

There is a perversion here, but it is not the one perceived by the mother. Human existence, both past and present, is filled with stories of motherlove. Daughters may be selfish, sons may be abusive, but mothers continue to love their children. Fatherlove is often perceived and portrayed as having a price attached. Working hard and being successful may earn fatherlove, but motherlove has been the model of unconditional love. Murderers, even serial killers, have been executed in the sight of a mother weeping for her little child lost. Yet here is a mother denouncing her daughter, a daughter who had not abused or murdered anyone, a daughter who was hard working and successful in her career, a daughter faithful to her partner, but her partner was someone of the same sex. Does this act define the limits of motherlove?

Parental rejection is the reason many argue that homophobia is the worst kind of prejudice because it can even turn family members against each other. Those who suffer from the actions of prejudiced people know they can always go home, that they can count on their family to welcome them and to love them and to help heal the hurt caused by others. Only gay men and lesbians may find that even their own families can harbor such homophobia that they will not be a harbor against the storm. The family may refuse to offer any comfort or compassion. It should surprise no one that drug and alcohol abuse have been major problems for many gay men and lesbians. Many people use drugs and alcohol to escape from pain.

One of the major components in viewing homosexuality as a perversion is that heterosexuals tend to focus on the sexual behavior of gay men and lesbians. Heterosexuality is usually viewed through the lens of love and intimacy and procreation, whereas homosexuality is usually viewed through the lens of lust and immorality and perversion. Human beings share common concerns and needs, and one need is to be loved and to express love in an intimate relationship. Another need is to respond to the sex drive, but sexual activity represents just one part of a person's life. During the day we eat and bathe and dress and undress and work and play and gossip and watch television and listen to music and read and write and think and celebrate. And then, as the poem says, "right in the middle of it/comes the smiling/mortician" [4, p. 89]. Why should sexual behavior alone be the basis for rejecting another human being?

Rejection . . . another story.

A lesbian couple worked in a medium sized city but wanted to live in a small town because both had been born and raised in small towns. They looked at houses in nearby communities and purchased an attractive home in a town close enough to the city to permit a comfortable commute to their jobs. Because both women had also been raised in evangelical families and retained their Christian faith, they hoped to find a church that would accept them. After attending several different services, they heard one minister who seemed broad minded and thoughtful so they went to see him. They explained that they would like to come to his church but they wanted him to be aware of their relationship. If lesbians were not welcome in his church, they would not intrude. He accepted them and encouraged them to attend the church he served.

After the two women had attended services for several months, the rumors began. The two women were living together; they bought their house together; they never seemed to go on dates nor did they bring men into their home. People wondered if they were lesbians, and in the time-tested tradition of gossip, the question became rhetorical. Everyone knew. One couple in the church was so convinced by the rumor that they came to see their minister. They told him it was well known in the community that these two women were lesbians and they demanded that he tell these women they were no longer welcome in the church.

The minister listened respectfully and when they finished he asked, "Are you saying that I should be concerned with the private sexual activities of my parishioners?" They nodded, that was exactly what they were saying. "All right," said the minister as he reached for his paper and pen, "Let's start with you. Tell me everything you enjoy doing sexually." Neither the husband nor his wife wanted to talk about that. "But you just told me I am supposed to be concerned with the sexual activities of my parishioners, so I am just doing what you say you want me to do." The couple still refused to discuss their sexual activities. "All right, so I guess you do not want me to poke my nose into what people do in their bedrooms." He put his pen and paper down. "And that's what I prefer as well." When the couple left his office that day they also left the church. No doubt they found another church which permitted them to persist in their prejudice.

The Christian church has played a major role in fanning the flames of homophobia for a long time. Literally. The medieval Christian church condoned burning men and women to death who were guilty of being attracted to people of the same sex. Sometimes they were accused of being heretics or witches, but such wickedness often included betraying their nature, heterosexuality being considered the only sexual orientation that was natural. When men were burned they were often bound tightly with ropes which gave them the appearance of tightly tied bundles of kindling called fagots. According to some scholars, the pejorative term "faggot" was crafted in these flames of faith and hatred [5, p. 138], creating another chapter in a history of atrocities committed by a religion whose fundamental principles are love and mercy and forgiveness, but whose leaders and followers have promoted and engaged in anti-Semitism, misogyny, and slavery.

In 1997, the Southern Baptist Church confessed that it had defended and legitimized slavery before the Civil War. The Church issued a formal proclamation apologizing for their mistake, but these same Southern Baptists were also denouncing the Disney Corporation and sponsoring a boycott of Disney for having gay friendly policies such as providing benefits for people in domestic partnerships. How long will it be before we can expect the next apology?

Why do people calling themselves Christians feel justified in maintaining this prejudice? There is very little mention of homosexuality in the Bible, and even where it seems to be condemned one must cautiously consider the context. The concept of homosexuality—having a persistent erotic attraction for someone of the same sex—is of relatively recent origin. The term was first coined in the middle of the nineteenth century and did not gain popular usage until the twentieth century. Previously, most Western societies had simply assumed that men and women were heterosexual by nature. When Biblical writers denounced men sleeping with men, they were chastizing heterosexual men for going against their nature and for wasting their procreative potential by "spilling their seed" on infertile ground. They were exhorting men to reject this perversion of their nature and to behave the way a heterosexual man should behave. This is not a condemnation of homosexuality but of heterosexuals engaging in inappropriate sexual activity [6]. With this in mind, one can argue that the Bible says nothing about homosexuality given what we now understand about sexual orientation.

Scientists still have much work to do to determine the genetic basis of sexual orientation and how it is influenced during fetal development and early childhood, but there is little support for the claim that being sexually attracted exclusively to members of the opposite sex is the natural orientation. Animal studies, as well as human history, clearly reveal the persistence of sexual activity among same sex participants as a naturally occurring phenomenon. Many homosexuals report having strong feelings of sexual attraction for people of the same sex early in their lives. Lesbians had "crushes" on favorite female teachers while their girl friends were having the same feelings for favorite male teachers. Gay men heard their teenage peers fantasizing about the latest cinema sex symbol while they were dreaming about handsome male actors.

Such self-reports, along with other evidence, support Alfred Kinsey's bell shaped curve of human sexuality which suggests that some people are born with a strong inclination toward being exclusively attracted to members of the same sex, just as others on the opposite end of the continuum are exclusively attracted to members of the opposite sex [7, p. 140]. Kinsey argues that the majority of people have a mixture of feelings but in a society that emphasizes heterosexuality, people feel pressured to reject any feelings of attraction toward members of the same sex.

If it's true that a certain percentage of people are born with a sexuality oriented exclusively toward homosexuality, then it makes no sense to persecute homosexuals on the basis of having made bad moral choices. There are gay men and lesbians who insist that they didn't choose to be homosexual, that they were born this way. Many people reject this idea because to accept it means they must recognize homophobia for what it is: a prejudice. Some Christian churches staunchly resist the claim of many gay men and lesbians that "God made me this way" because it compels them to question conventional beliefs about the Creator and the nature of the Creation.

Some Christians accept the idea that homosexuality is innate and not a choice, but still insist that homosexual behavior is a sin. They exhort gay men and lesbians to resist temptations to engage in homosexual activity, to be celibate or try to find satisfaction in heterosexual activity. They say the homosexual orientation is a test from God. Why God should concoct such a test and assign it only to a certain percentage of people is not clear, nor is it clear why the sin of homosexuality is so abominable. A thief deprives a person of rewards earned; a murderer deprives a person of life; a homosexual loves and cares for another person who happens to be of the same sex. And the sin is . . .?

If Americans accepted the idea that some people are born with a sexual attraction exclusively for same sex partners, would that eliminate homophobia in our society? Probably not. People could use Kinsey's studies to argue that most people have a bisexual orientation which means they have the capacity for engaging in homosexual activities, but they can make a choice. The arguments in support of encouraging people to reject homosexual activities and be exclusively heterosexual would range from religious to pragmatic, but they would be grounded in the idea that there is a choice to be made and the choice affects the entire society.

What is this choice? It is a choice about a person to love and making love with that person. What moral or ethical principles should be upheld? Someone who wants to maintain traditional values could advocate for the principles historically used for heterosexual relationships by exhorting all couples, whether in marriages or domestic partnerships, to be loving and kind and generous and faithful. Since society's mores now recognize that people make mistakes and allow heterosexual couples to divorce and marry someone else, the same allowance should be given to same sex couples in domestic partnerships. Since our society now takes a more permissive attitude toward premarital sexual activity among heterosexuals, it should take the same kind of attitude toward such activity among gay men and lesbians.

If someone chooses to be involved in a homosexual relationship, that is no excuse for hatred or prejudice. People make many personal choices in life, but should any choices be considered a legitimate basis for perpetuating prejudice and animosity? Consider the following:

Is it acceptable for North Dakotans to be suspicious of a New Yorker who chooses to move to Bismark?

Is it acceptable for Protestants to condemn a Lutheran who chooses to convert to Catholicism?

Is it acceptable for Caucasians to denounce a white woman who chooses to marry a black man?

Is it acceptable for Christians to hate the Jews for choosing not to acknowledge Jesus Christ as the Messiah?

The problem is not the choice but our response to the choice. Our response to homosexuality is to hate and fear it. Our response to homosexuality is homophobia.

Homosexuality is not the perversion, homophobia is. It perverts the family by sowing seeds of rejection and hostility which tears families apart. It perverts Christianity by turning the Christians who are supposed to love everyone, even their enemies, into people who hate. It perverts our humanity by diminishing our compassion for other human beings. For proof of this, consider the issue of gay bashing. Most attacks are unprovoked. The gay basher assaults his victim simply because he believes the victim is homosexual. In the vast majority of cases the gay basher is a teenage male, apparently so insecure about his own sexuality that he needs to attack a gay man to prove his masculinity to himself and to others. Reports from schools document that students are verbally harassed and even physically attacked if they are perceived to be homosexual. Where is the source of the problem? By any standard of justice and decency, whose behavior is perverse?

Once I discussed this issue for over two hours with a young man who was a fundamentalist Christian. He did not to want to condemn homosexuals but he believed the Bible left him no choice. We discussed Old Testament rejections of abominations and New Testament admonitions to love and forgive. How to reconcile the two? Near the end of our conversation we agreed that it didn't matter whether or not we had the same interpretation of what the Bible said about homosexuality, but we could agree on other passages, "Why do you see the speck that is in your brother's eye, but do not notice the log that is in your own eye" (Matthew 7:3)? "Judge not lest ye be judged" (Luke 6:7). In these passages and many more, Christians are encouraged to behave toward others in ways that reflect God's love and mercy and compassion. For human beings to judge others is a usurpation of God's role. Most religions agree that human beings should not judge others but should look for ways to improve themselves. When one human being judges another, that implies that this individual can make judgments as well as God. It is an act of arrogance. Such judgments ignore Paul's unequivocal assertion that human beings can only see "through the glass darkly" (Corinthians 13:12).

Homophobia will continue to affect all of us until some of us stand up and name it for what it is—a perversion of the human spirit. Homophobia will continue to produce prejudice and hatred in our society until institutions and corporations and government agencies declare it unacceptable and refuse to sanction it. Homophobia will receive a mortal blow when religious leaders of all faiths discard their sermons on the evils of homosexuality and persuade their followers that the universal call for compassion should be answered every day and that no human being should be excluded from that compassion.

Is this mortal blow forthcoming? Instead of promoting understanding and empathy, many religious leaders are silenced by the power of ancient prejudices still strong among the masses of people. As this society struggles to overcome homophobia, that struggle should be viewed as a litmus test for measuring our compassion. The extent to which each of us is prepared to resist and reject the forces that demonize those who are different, the extent to which we do not allow differences to divide us, is the extent to which we extend our vision of humanity to include all of those who are here and who belong here . . . beside us . . . and among us.

# CHAPTER SIX
## In the Key of F: FORGIVENESS

### LA GUARDIA'S JUDGMENT

During his tenure as Mayor of New York, Fiorello La Guardia would occasionally preside at the police court. On one occasion it was a bitterly cold day and the elderly man brought before La Guardia was charged with stealing a loaf of bread. Asked why he had become a thief at his age, the trembling old man said his family was starving. "I've got to punish you," La Guardia told him. "The law makes no exceptions. I can do nothing but sentence you to a fine of ten dollars.

At this point La Guardia reached into his own pocket, pulled out some dollar bills then held up a ten dollar bill saying, "Here's the ten dollars to pay your fine." The old man was too astonished to take the money so La Guardia added, "And now, I remit the fine." With that he threw the ten dollar bill into his famous sombrero. "Furthermore," he went on, "I'm going to fine everybody in this courtroom fifty cents for living in a town where a man has to steal bread in order to eat. Mr. Bailiff, collect the fines and give them to this defendant." The sombrero was passed around and the incredulous old man left the courtroom with a stake of forty-seven dollars and fifty cents [1, p. 339].

> **Forgiveness**—absolving another of a debt . . . granting free pardon for an offense or to an offender . . . ceasing to feel resentment against another.

Forgiveness began as a money matter. To forgive another was to say to that person—you do not have to repay the money you owe me. To forgive someone was serious business. Eventually the word was used to excuse people from a broader array of offenses beyond that of owing a debt, but the magnanimous principle behind the act remained the same: it lifted some burden from another. It was a grant of freedom. This was not merely a figurative freedom but could be a literal one since it might mean keeping the offender from going to jail or liberating a person already incarcerated.

As the word evolved, it expanded to include one of the most difficult ethical practices of all: *to cease feeling resentment toward the offender*. It is one thing to forgive a debt, it is quite another to forgive the debtor. There are situations where it might be relatively easy, even pragmatic, to forgive a debt. One could loan money to finance a project that fails, leaving the debtor so hopelessly in debt that it is not likely this person will ever be able to repay the loan. In such circumstances, the impression made on others by a charitable decision to forgive the debt may be worth as much as the money lost. In such circumstances the debt might be forgiven, but the forgiveness might not extend to the debtor. One could go to the grave bearing animosity toward the individual whose failure created this problem. To forgive the offender as well as the offense is an act of astonishing generosity.

Martin Luther King, Jr. was an articulate advocate of forgiveness. While encouraging people to work for the goal of freedom from oppression, King exhorted his followers to be nonviolent and to forgive those behaving violently toward them. King said, "Forgiveness does not mean ignoring what has been done or putting a false label on an evil act . . . Forgiveness is a catalyst creating the atmosphere necessary for a fresh start . . . It is the lifting of a burden or the canceling of a debt" [2, pp. 48-49]. In the Christian spirit of loving one's enemies, King refused to hate the white people who hated him. To those expressing their venomous hatred, not only toward him but toward the Civil Rights movement, King had this response:

> We shall match your capacity to inflict suffering by our capacity to endure . . . Do to us what you will, and we shall continue to love you. We cannot in all good conscience obey your unjust laws, because nonco-operation with evil is as much a moral obligation as is co-operation with good. Throw us in jail, and we shall still love you. Send your hooded perpetrators of violence into our community at the midnight hour and beat us and leave us half dead, and we shall still love you. But be ye assured that we will wear you down by our capacity to suffer [2, pp. 54-55].

Other African Americans expressed similar sentiments during the Civil Rights struggle, and their beliefs were reflected in their behavior during marches and other protest activities. This spirit of forgiveness was perhaps best exemplified by Mamie Mobley, mother of Emmet Till. Till was the fourteen-year-old Black youth brutally murdered for being "too friendly" with a white woman in Mississippi. Although her son's killers were acquitted by an all white jury, Mobley refused to be bitter. In one interview she said, "I did not wish them dead. I did not wish them in jail." She insisted it was not her job to punish them for what they had done, and "it was not for me to go around hugging hate to myself because hate would destroy me." When Mobley was asked how she felt about the two men who had mutilated and murdered her only child, she replied:

> I had no feeling whatsoever toward (them) . . . If I had to, I could take their four little children . . . and I could raise those children as if they were my own and I could have loved them . . . I haven't spent one night hating those people. I have not looked at a white person (as) an enemy [3, p. 21].

This is not the normal response for most people; the normal response is to pass judgment on others and act accordingly. This response is incorporated into our sense of justice expressed in the principle of making the punishment fit the crime. Being fair, or at least perceived as fair, is important. We don't want to punish someone too harshly who committed a minor offense, but we don't want someone who committed a major offense to receive only a mild punishment.

---

**Judgment**—based on careful weighing of evidence and testing of premises, making objective decisions from circumstances presented . . . passing sentence on someone . . . a divine sentence (a misfortune inflicted by God) . . . the final judging of mankind by God.

---

Like forgiveness, judgment is a principle that originates with money; therefore it is taken just as seriously. A judgment is a judicial decision which mandates that the debtor must pay what is owed, and such a judgment clearly casts aspersions on the debtor's character. From such a beginning it was inevitable that the term would evolve from the judicial to the personal. People make judgments about others, and many will insist that they are being totally objective, that they consider all the evidence and weigh all the arguments, but in the end they pass sentence by concluding that the other is good or bad, wise or foolish, friend or foe.

It is not surprising that the concept of judgment would ultimately be accorded to a divine judge. For years, people from various faiths interpreted misfortunes as punishments attesting to divine displeasure. Jonathan Edwards vividly described the fate of "sinners in the hands of an angry God," and their fate was not fortuitous [4]. Such attitudes provide a foundation for our sense of fairness. We say people should get what they deserve, receive their *just desserts*. Such judgments are not restricted to individuals but can be pronounced on groups. Some say poor people lack the proper values to be successful. Some denounce welfare recipients as lazy and immoral; many reject gay men as promiscuous and perverted. Passing judgment seems to make people feel good, perhaps even god-like, and certainly powerful.

Going against the tide of this human propensity for judgment is a body of literature from philosophers and humanists and spiritual leaders telling us that making judgments is unwise, that forgiving others nurtures the human spirit and strengthens the bonds within the human community. To err is human and to forgive is the divine but difficult path we are urged to take, an obligatory path for those who follow in the footsteps of Christ.

Whether or not one is a Christian or even religious, forgiveness should still be considered essential if we are to resolve the dilemmas that divide us. Mayor La Guardia went to the police court to sit in judgment over others. His judgment satisfied the letter of the law, but his forgiveness satisfied a higher law. His judgment showed a proper concern for enforcing the law but even more proper was his compassion for the plight of a starving man with no money for food. His judgment called on the others in the courtroom to take responsibility for the old man's suffering. His judicial decision had more of forgiveness than judgment in it.

Pronouncing judgment is often an act of arrogance, an assumption of power over others which can have destructive, even catastrophic consequences. Adolf Hitler, Heinrich Himmler, and a handful of German National Socialists passed judgment on the Jews and disseminated their decision to a receptive audience. Many Germans had already made such a judgment; therefore, the Nazi bigotry merely confirmed the verdict of the majority. The result of this collective judgment in Poland and Austria as well as Germany was a tragedy whose dimensions we still struggle to comprehend.

"Never forget" is the message of the Jews who survived the concentration camps. It is not only based on a desire to honor the memory of those who died, but to learn the lessons that this tragedy teaches. One of the lessons of the Holocaust is to recognize the consequences for any society when forgiveness and tolerance is despised as weak and cowardly and the assertion of one's right to judge others and to punish those perceived as inferior is regarded as the more worthy goal. Forgiveness may not be easy, especially the forgiveness that comes from the heart, but we have been given a powerful example of the alternative. If we never forget this example of judgment and the injustice inflicted upon millions, if we keep the images from the Holocaust vividly in our minds, it should be difficult to find someone to cast the first stone.

## HEARING VOICES

*And when ye stand praying, forgive, if you
have aught against any; that your Father
also which is in heaven may forgive you
your trespasses. But if ye do not forgive,
neither will your Father which is in heaven
forgive your trespasses."*
                                    Mark (11:25-26)

*A kind speech and forgiveness is better
than alms followed by injury.*
                                    Qur'an (Sura 2:260)

*No man can justly censure or condemn
another, because indeed no man truly
knows another.*
                                    Sir Thomas Browne

*We hand folks over to God's mercy, and
show none ourselves.*
                                    George Eliot

*. . . in the course of justice none of us
Should see salvation: we do pray for mercy,
And that same prayer doth teach us all to render
The deeds of mercy.*
                                    William Shakespeare

*It is easier to forgive an enemy than to
forgive a friend.*
                                    William Blake

*'Tis not the dying for a faith that's so hard . . .
'tis the living up to it that is difficult.*
                                    William Makepeace Thackeray

*'Twas a thief said the last kind word to Christ:
Christ took the kindness and forgave the theft.*
                                    Robert Browning

*If Jesus Christ were to come today,
people would not even crucify him.
They would ask him to dinner, and hear
what he had to say, and make fun of it.*
                                    Thomas Carlyle

*They would have been equally horrified*
*at hearing the Christian religion doubted,*
*and at seeing it practised.*

Samuel Butler

> *A man should never be ashamed to own*
> *he has been in the wrong, which is but*
> *saying . . . that he is wiser to-day than*
> *he was yesterday.*
>
> Alexander Pope

*We should look long and carefully at*
*ourselves before we pass judgment*
*on others.*

Jean Baptiste Moliere

> *Use every man after his desert, and*
> *who should 'scape whipping?*
>
> William Shakespeare

*Our deeds determine us, as much as we*
*determine our deeds.*

George Eliot

> *Only the brave know how to forgive . . .*
> *A coward never . . . It's not in his*
> *nature.*
>
> Laurence Sterne

*All wars are civil wars, because all men*
*are brothers . . . Each one owes infinitely*
*more to the human race than to the*
*particular country in which he was*
*born.*

Francois Fenelon

> *Here lie I, Martin Elginbrodde:*
> *Hae mercy o' my soul, Lord God,;*
> *As I wad do, were I Lord God,*
> *And ye were Martin Elginbrodde.*
>
> George MacDonald

*God will pardon me. It is His job.*

Heinrich Heine

## THE WISDOM OF FORGIVENESS

To get wisdom is better than gold.
Proverbs 16:16 [5]

He giveth wisdom to whom He will:
and  he to whom wisdom is given,
hath had much good given him . . .
Qur'an (Sura 2:270) [6]

The wisdom literature of Judaism and other ancient religions is filled with advice on how to be wise, how to be righteous, how to find the straight path and how to avoid the crooked. Some advice is quite specific and pragmatic:

If you have found honey, eat only
enough for you
lest you be sated with it and
vomit it.
Proverbs 25:16

Other advice is implied in a general lamentation regarding the human condition:

Again I saw all the oppressions that are practiced under the sun. And behold, the tears of the oppressed, and there was no one to comfort them!
Ecclesiastes 4:1

What does the wisdom literature have to say about the wisdom of forgiveness? Does the wise person forgive or demand judgment? Is the forgiving person wise or gullible? Studying the wisdom literature of the Hebrew scriptures, it is apparent that the poet was right, to forgive is divine. In Psalms, Proverbs, and the prophets, God's forgiveness is frequently implored and gratitude is expressed by those who assume that they personally, or the Jews as a people, have been granted God's forgiveness. If God is a role model for humanity, then forgiveness is divine and represents an action human beings should emulate.

In the New Testament forgiveness is repeatedly advocated. People are to forgive others as God forgives them. Jesus teaches his followers a prayer which asks for forgiveness of our debts "as we forgive our debtors." After Christ's death the apostle Paul reminds Christians of their obligations: "Forbearing one another, and forgiving one another, if any man have a quarrel against another; even as Christ forgave you, so also do ye" [Colossians 3:13). Forgiveness is frequently encouraged in the Bible, but what is said about forgiveness in other religions?

Confucius does not refer to forgiveness directly, but in his emphasis on self-improvement, he challenges his followers to focus on their own behaviors rather than judging others. "Attack the evil that is within yourself, do not attack the evil that is in others" [Book 12:21] [7]. The advice Confucius offers is not about forgiving others but withholding judgment of others while accepting the responsibility to improve one's own ethical behavior. "To have faults and to be making no effort to mend them is to have faults indeed" [Book 15:29]. When Confucius is told that one of his disciples, Tzu-Kung, has frequently been heard to make negative judgments of others, the Master offers this gentle rebuke, "It is fortunate for Tzu-Kung that he is so perfect himself as to have time to spare for this. I myself have none" [Book 14:31].

Arguing the need for self-improvement does not provide clear guidance about how to behave toward others. It should not be difficult to refrain from criticism, but how are others to be treated, especially those whose behavior is not above reproach? Confucius' response is to offer a form of the Golden Rule, "Do not do to others what you would not like yourself" [Book 12:2]. The wisdom of Confucius does not demand that people do good to everyone they encounter; instead, like Hippocrates, Confucius merely suggests that they "do no harm." Although forgiveness is not the specific theme, refraining from judgment and retribution is clearly advocated.

This is analogous to Buddhism which promotes the eightfold path as the way to deal with the distractions and destructions of daily life. One follows the eightfold path in search of the enlightenment achieved by Gautama Siddhartha, the Buddha. This enlightenment includes rejection of judgment and violent punishment as illustrated in the story of Asoka, the great emperor of Magadha in Northern India.

As he began his reign, Asoka ruled with a savagery that matched his predecessors. At his capital (now called Patna), there was a fearful prison called "Asoka's Hell" from which, the emperor decreed, no one should leave alive. A follower of Buddha, wrongly accused of a crime, was arrested and sent to this prison. When torturers threw him into a cauldron of boiling water, he was not harmed. After the jailer informed the emperor of this miracle, Asoka came to the prison to see for himself.

The emperor ordered the jailer to prepare the cauldron of boiling water again and to throw the Buddhist into it. Once again the man was not harmed. Asoka was astonished and disturbed. As the emperor prepared to leave, the jailer reminded Asoka of his own edict that no one was to leave the prison alive. This comment so enraged Asoka that he gave orders for the jailer to be thrown into the cauldron. The jailer did not leave the prison alive.

Asoka's experience in prison affected him deeply. Not long after this, he embraced Buddhism and ordered the prison demolished. As he continued his rule, Asoka erected pillars on which his edicts were carved to provide testimony to his humanity, to document his concern that justice and mercy be shown to all his subjects, animal as well as human [8].

Do no harm. It is one of the consistent exhortations of the wisdom literature, but this is not the same as forgiveness. Do other religions urge believers to forgive others their faults?

Religions of many indigenous people include the need to ask for and be granted forgiveness. This principle is often extended to animals. The nomadic Nemadi of Mauritania roam the western part of the Sahara Desert hunting antelope with small packs of trained dogs. One dog lunges for the antelope's neck while the others attack its legs. As soon as the dogs have brought their prey down, the hunter moves in to kill it with his knife. As the animal dies, the hunter utters a brief prayer asking the animal for forgiveness [9].

This Nemadi practice is analogous to a ritual prayer practiced by many Native Americans. Whereas the Nemadi prayer is brief, the Native American hunter may include an explanation as part of the request for forgiveness. Consider this Anishnabeg prayer to a slain deer:

I had need.

I have dispossessed you of beauty,
    grace, and life.
I have sundered your spirit
    from its worldly frame.
No more will you run in
    freedom
Because of my need.

I had need.
You have in life
    served your kind
    in goodness.
By your life I will
    serve my brothers.
Without you I hunger
    and grow weak.
Without you I am
    helpless, nothing.

I had need.

> Give me your flesh
>    for strength.
> Give me your casement
>    for protection.
> Give me your bones for my labors,
>    and I shall not want.

Hinduism embraces other religions by perceiving them as many paths to the same God. Hinduism affirms the spiritual truths proclaimed by other religions and offers its own insights into the wisdom of forgiveness. Hinduism views forgiveness much like the Hebrew scriptures, asking God for forgiveness rather than admonishing men to forgive one another. There is a Hindu prayer which is frequently spoken before the beginning of worship in the temple. The prayer is so well-known it can be heard even in the temples of small villages, and it illustrates not only Hinduism's perspective on forgiveness but also on humility:

> O Lord, forgive three sins that are due to my human limitations:
>    Thou art everywhere, but I worship you here;
>    Thou art without form, but I worship you in these forms;
>    Thou needest no praise, yet I offer you these prayers and salutations;
> Lord, forgive three sins that are due to my human limitations [10, p. 42].

This prayer also illustrates why Hinduism accepts other religions. All religions attempt to worship the same inscrutable and unknowable God. Hinduism recognizes the inability of human beings to fully comprehend God, and asks for forgiveness for an inability which is characteristic of all humans. For this reason, Hindus are taught to accept believers from other faiths, as illustrated in this excerpt from the writings of Ramakrishna:

> There was a man who worshipped Shiva but hated all other deities. One day Shiva appeared to him and said, "I shall never be pleased with thee so long as thou hatest the other gods." But the man was inexorable. After a few days Shiva again appeared to him and said, "I shall never be pleased with thee so long as thou hatest." The man kept silent. After a few days Shiva again appeared to him. This time one side of his body was that of Shiva, and the other side that of Vishnu. The man was half pleased and half displeased. He laid his offering on the side representing Shiva, and did not offer anything to the side representing Vishnu. Then Shiva said, "Thy bigotry is unconquerable. I, by assuming this dual aspect, tried to convince thee that all gods and goddesses are but various aspects of the one Absolute Brahmin" [10, pp. 87-88].

This story promotes harmony rather than hatred toward the various ways to worship God, yet religious bigotry has been common in human affairs. History amply documents the fact that people of one faith have been unforgiving and unaccepting of other faiths. As Jonathan Swift wrote, "We have just enough religion to make us hate, but not enough to make us love one another" [11, p. 241]. The word bigot was originally a slur coined by the French to insult Normans in the twelfth century. The word, but not the hate it represented, disappeared until the fifteenth century when a Middle English phrase, "bi god" was used as an epithet for someone perceived to be a religious fanatic or superstitious hypocrite. The English usage reminded the French of their older insult and it was revived as "bigoterie" which became "bigotry" when the English adopted it [12, p. 259]. It is appropriate that its English origins had a religious basis since religion has been and continues to be an obstacle to peace between nations and among the diverse faiths within nations.

In recent years, Muslims have been branded as religious bigots and fanatics due to terrorist actions committed by extremists and the ongoing conflict between Israel and several Islamic nations. But Christians have not viewed themselves as religious bigots despite the bombings and killings at abortion clinics by extremists and the centuries of conflict between Protestants and Catholics in Ireland. It is important to put these negative perceptions of Muslims in a broader context as we look to the Qur'an for its insights concerning forgiveness.

Muslims believe that the Hebrew scriptures are a truthful account of God's relationship with the Jews, and they accept Jesus as one of the many prophets of God, but Muhammed is seen as the culmination of those who have revealed God's will to us. Muhammed brought the final revelation of truth to the world and most Muslims believe there will be no more prophets after him. What is the place of forgiveness in Muhammed's final revelation of truth?

Because of the term "jihad" (often translated as "holy war") and the historical record of Muslim military conquests, especially in the first century after Muhammed's death, one might assume that Islam is intolerant of competing faiths and sanctions the use of violence against nonbelievers; but, we should remember that the medieval Christian Crusades were an attempt to crush the Muslim infidel for the greater glory of God. It is true that the Qur'an permits warfare, but only in two forms: as a defense against invaders or as an action to right a wrong. Offensive wars are forbidden because "God hateth the aggressor" (Sura

2:180). The Qur'an also tells Muslims to respect God's relationship with Jews and Christians:

> We believe in God, and that which hath been sent down to us, and that which hath been sent down to Abraham and Ismael and Isaac and Jacob and the tribes: and that which hath been given to Moses and to Jesus, and that which was given to the prophets from their Lord. No difference do we make between any of them . . . [Sura 2:130].

Although the Qur'an does not forbid judgment nor demands for retribution, it encourages believers to forgive. The following passage instructs Muslims that the retribution exacted for an injury should not exceed the injury—an eye for an eye—but to forgive the other is to be rewarded with God's love, a powerful incentive:

> And who, when a wrong is done them, redress themselves: Yet let the recompense of evil be only a like evil—but he who forgiveth and is reconciled, shall be rewarded by God himself; for He loveth not those who act unjustly [Sura 42:40].

As with most of the world's major religions, there are diverse perspectives within Islam. One particular sect of Sunni Muslims called Murjites adamantly maintain that only God should judge human beings:

> (Murjites), believing that not men, but only Allah can judge a man's true intentions, refuse to condemn men who appear to be sinners. They believe that judgment upon disbelievers and other evildoers remains God's province and beyond the wisdom of imperfect men [1, p. 328].

Are there any conclusions about the wisdom of forgiveness that can be drawn from this brief foray into diverse religious traditions? All of these religions appear to agree on the need to refrain from judging others, but this does not necessarily include forgiveness. They simply urge believers not to judge the faults of others but to focus on their own faults. Christianity seems to be the only religion openly advocating that its believers forgive the sins of others in the hope that their sins will be forgiven by God, but there is a paradox in this. Like the other religions, Christians are instructed not to judge others, and yet to perceive someone as a sinner needing forgiveness is to make a judgment. It is as if Jesus realized that human beings would not be able to refrain from judging others, and in anticipation of this failure he required them to forgive their fellow sinners.

There appears to be a consensus among monotheistic faiths that all human beings fall short of perfection; therefore, forgiveness is a favor devoutly desired from a merciful God. Only God has the power, and the responsibility, to reward the faithful, condemn the nonbeliever, and forgive those who believe but fail to be faithful to God's commands. Forgiveness is portrayed as a divine attribute; therefore, one could assume that human beings ought to behave similarly toward others as they hope God will behave toward them.

Understanding words of wisdom does not make it easy to follow them. Forgiving another can be difficult. Perhaps we should begin with those we love. We should be able to forgive them even when we think they do not deserve forgiveness, even when they are indisputably wrong and we are indisputably right (and justifiably angry). And yet it may be harder to forgive those you love because so much more is expected from them. When they fail us, the pain of their failure is intensified by the sense of betrayal. How could they do that to me? How can I ever forgive them! Forgiving the flaws of a stranger may seem far simpler since it does not involve the powerful emotions aroused by love and kinship. No matter how it is done, forgiveness must be practiced. A forgiving nature does not develop merely by admiring this virtue in others.

No matter what faith one believes, or if one rejects all faiths, there is a universal rationale for forgiveness. Whatever standards of moral conduct are proclaimed in any society, history proves that human beings will fail to meet them. This does not mean we should cease striving to achieve our ideals, but we should not judge others harshly for failing to measure up. It is also important that people forgive themselves for their flaws and failures if they want to achieve peace of mind. Such serenity may help in contemplating the complexity of life and the mystery of death while people struggle to find reasons to be comforted and hopeful. Forgiving ourselves and others gives us permission to seek the perfection just beyond our reach, to stare through the glass darkly and not be deceived by the illusion that the glass is only a mirror.

ಋ ಋ ಋ

## ECHOES

*The discoverer of the role of*
*forgiveness in the realm of human*
*affairs was Jesus of Nazareth.*
Hannah Arendt

*It is a cardinal principle of*
*Judeo-Christian ethics that forgiveness*
*must always be granted to the sincerely*
*repentant.*
Edward Flannery

*The Christian ideal has not been*
*tried and found wanting. It has been*
*found difficult; and left untried.*
G. K. Chesterton

*The faith in which I was brought up*
*assured me that I was better than other*
*people; I was saved and they were*
*damned. Our hymns were loaded with*
*arrogance—self congratulations on how*
*cozy we were with the Almighty and what*
*a high opinion He had of us and what*
*hell everybody else would catch come*
*judgment day.*
Robert Heinlein

*A Christian is a man who feels*
*Repentance on a Sunday*
*For what he did on Saturday*
*And is going to do on Monday.*
Thomas Russell Ybarra

*To be social is to be forgiving.*
Robert Frost

*Without forgiveness, life is governed*
*by an endless cycle of resentment*
*and retaliation.*
Roberto Assagioli

*Forgiveness is the true foundation of
health and happiness, just as it is for
lasting progress. Without forgiveness
there is no forgetfulness of evil; without
forgetfulness there still remains the
threat of violence. And violence does not
solve anything; it only prolongs itself.*
                        Alice Walker

*. . . to understand is to forgive . . .*
                        Miguel de Unamuno

*To be forgiven is to feel free to step into the
future unburdened by the precedent of who
we have been and what we have done . . .
liberating ourselves from the idea that we
are still who we used to be, and freeing
ourselves to become a new person.*
                        Harold Kushner

*(It was) my mother's wish for my brother
and me, that we learn how to understand,
and . . . how to forgive: understand the
mistakes and errors of our ways . . . (and)
forgive ourselves, lest we give our errant
or evil side the continuing hold over us
that such a refusal of forgiveness all too
commonly, readily ensures.*

                        Robert Coles

*I can never forgive myself for recklessly
and unscrupulously supporting a regime
that carried out the systematic murder of
Jews and (others). My moral guilt is not
subject to the statute of limitations; it
cannot be erased in my lifetime.*
                        Albert Speer

*God shall forgive thee all but thy despair.*
                        Christopher Hollis

*Forgiveness is the imitation of God.
Punishment too is an imitation of God.
God punishes and forgives, in that order.
But God never hates.*
                        Hans Habe

## OF LAST THOUGHTS AND APPLE EATING

But where shall wisdom be found?
and where is the place of understanding? [Job (28:12)].

Job's questions are fundamental to the search for wisdom and understanding. A lifetime isn't long; we all need assistance in the journey
toward wisdom. To be told where wisdom resides, or at least the right
direction to take, is helpful even though it does not guarantee success.
We also have to recognize wisdom when we find it. Religions claim that
wisdom resides in their holy books. One does not have to embrace the
faith to recognize the truths these books contain, but even believers
struggle to understand the wisdom offered there, and understanding
does not necessarily make one wise. Wisdom is reflected not in the
expression of ideas but in the choices one makes which reflect those
ideas. To make choices which contradict the beliefs one espouses is to
engage in hypocrisy as illustrated by a professor of ethics who insisted
he only taught the subject and didn't have to practice its principles
[14, p. 182].

This is one of many contradictions confronting teachers. Teaching
is part of a tradition of human service, yet arrogance is inherent in
teaching. Teachers demand an enormous amount of time from children
and youth who do not yet know how many years of life they have before
them. Students are asked to believe that what teachers say and what
they require of students is so important and so valuable that their lives
will be enriched and improved by these experiences. This is the
unspoken but arrogant assertion of formal education. The aspiration to
fulfill the promise implicit in this assertion is one that only the best and
most committed teachers will strive to achieve. They will do so with
deepest humility, recognizing that they cannot possibly achieve the goal
with every student.

One of my favorite teachers once said that the best way to learn
about living was to learn about dying. With that in mind, I read books
that described what people said when they knew they were dying. Some
approached death with the same wit and charm that characterized their
lives. According to one biographer, Gertrude Stein's last words were,
"What is the answer? . . . In that case, what is the question?" As the poet
Heinrich Heine lay on his deathbed he was asked how he would justify
his life to God, and he responded, "God will pardon me. It is His job."
Some people reflect on their lives and regret actions not taken or words
not spoken. For others, this final judgment is not an assessment of
material wealth but an attempt to understand what life has meant and
what they have accomplished. Most of these last judgments become

ethical reflections on what has been learned, on the wisdom gained not the wealth.

Do people always gain wisdom from life experiences? Nathaniel Hawthorne responded to this question in a short story about elderly people being given a chance to drink a liquid which would make them young again [15]. Prior to drinking, all of the people seemed to understand the follies of their youth and to regret them, but after drinking they forget what they had learned in the thrill of seeing themselves young again. Were they to stay young, it is clear that all of them would commit the same mistakes as before. Hawthorne's response, however, is not consistent with what I have learned from talking to elderly people.

Some have expressed words of wisdom wrestled from a life of pain and struggle; others have achieved a kind of serenity which may be admirable yet difficult to emulate; others have affirmed Hawthorne's pessimism by maintaining their prejudices and misperceptions. This diversity has sustained my interest in the perspectives of people approaching the end of life. I like to read the last book ever written by an author I admire. I enjoy listening to people who are living in the twilight of their lives.

At some universities, professors are invited to give a "last lecture" before retiring. How do they sum up what they have learned in a lifetime of looking and listening and reading and thinking and feeling? How do they make sense of the random events in their lives: coping with pain or bouyed by joy; brought down by despair or soaring with success? How do they analyze it and sort it all out and turn it into advice for those who feel lost or defeated and who are looking for footsteps to follow?

During the turbulent decade of the 1960s, we were surrounded by slogans appearing on buttons and bumper stickers and bulletin boards such as, "If you're not part of the solution you're part of the problem." One slogan always puzzled me: "Today is the first day of the rest of your life." What did that mean? If people were to decide that it is best to live each day as if it were the first day of the rest of their lives, would they be justified in adopting a nonchalant attitude? If they made bad decisions which hurt others or if they engaged in irresponsible behavior, wouldn't there be ample time to atone for whatever mistakes they might make?

It would seem better for people to behave as though each day was the last day of their lives. This would demand a clear sense of purpose and an identified set of priorities. In the midst of a quarrel with a loved one, people who believed that today could be their last day alive might ask, "If I were never to see this person again, I will always be remembered by this quarrel. Is that how I want to be remembered?" Sometimes the answer will be "Yes" because the quarrel is based on an important aspect of the person's beliefs, but more often the quarrel probably stems from something petty and not worth prolonging.

The role of death in defining the significance of one's choices is presented dramatically in "The Mission," a film telling the story of two priests in the nineteenth century ministering to indigenous people in what is now Brazil. By the end of the film, the natives are being attacked by Portuguese soldiers. The priest who used to be a soldier rallies the men to fight while the other priest encourages nonviolent resistance. Each priest has his followers, but in the end it makes no difference. Everyone is slaughtered. For months I was haunted by that film, not because of the violence but as an apt metaphor for life. Each of us must make decisions about how we are going to live, but our fate is inescapable. Death offers no options.

This does not mean that the choices we make in life are meaningless or that life is futile given its inevitable ending. On the contrary, knowing that death awaits us does not trivialize life but enhances it. A belief in reincarnation may trivialize human life if it is used to argue that one should simply acquiesce in life's cruelties and accept unjust conditions because there will be other opportunities for a more satisfying experience. This reduces one's existence to a game of dice and dismisses the possibilities in each person's life. Although individual beliefs about reincarnation differ, its appeal to Americans appears to be based on its promise of an immortality that is individual and material rather than spiritual.

A greater reverence for life is expressed in the idea of human existence as ephemeral and transitory. This challenges the believer to live with an enthusiasm for life because death is, as e. e. cummings says, "(life's) rhythmic lover" [16, p. 6]. When Europeans first immigrated to the Western hemisphere they demonstrated their willingness to confront the reality of death. Visit an old cemetery in New England; carved on many stones one can find epitaphs and poetry which speak to us over the centuries of their awareness of death:

> Stranger, pause as you pass by,
> As you are now, so once was I,
> As I am now so you shall be.
> Prepare for death, and follow me.

Europeans today seem to maintain a consciousness of mortality which many Americans have abandoned. This consciousness is seen in subtle and obvious ways. One obvious example is the display of skeletons in European churches and cathedrals. There is an Austrian church famous for being the site of the wedding scene in the popular film, "The

Sound of Music." Encased in glass at the bottom of the altar are two skeletons, each lying on its side, one on the left of the altar and one on the right. Between and slightly above these two, positioned in the center of the altar, is yet another glass enclosed skeleton sitting upright on a throne, holding a scepter and facing forward as if greeting all those assembled before the altar. The expressions on the faces of several American tourists when I visited this church suggested that they were surprised and disturbed by the display. Some expressed disgust. One young woman wrinkled her nose as though smelling something foul and said, "How gross!"

Americans are not used to realistic displays of what happens to our bodies after we die, and even those who saw "The Sound of Music" were not prepared for this sight. In the film, the skeletons lying at the bottom of the altar cannot be recognized because of the distance of the camera from the altar. The skeleton in the center of the altar, which no camera angle could avoid, was covered by a full length portrait of Jesus. Apparently the filmmakers felt their audience would be offended by the sceptered skeleton intruding on the wedding. Perhaps they had American audiences in mind. In comparison, there is evidence that Europeans have historically accepted death as part of life. In Switzerland there is an ancient wooden bridge at Luzern with a series of drawings called "Totentanz" (dance of death) which portray skeletons in attendance at births, weddings, harvests, funerals, and other important events of life. The paintings portray death as ever present, not to inhibit life's celebrations but to make the celebration sweeter.

Too many Americans have lost this awareness, and it has been a grievous loss, all the more grievous because it is not grieved. We feel fortunate for its disappearance. Some put their faith in wrinkle creams and regular exercise, others in technology and transplants. Some race to the finish line refusing to recognize that we are the rabbit and time is the tortoise who is slowly overtaking us. At the finish line everyone is finished. The results are already recorded in the record books. We lose. Instead of racing against time, it would be better if we would take time to think about what we want to do with our lives, which path we want to take, recognizing that all paths end in the valley of the shadow of death. Such an awareness of mortality need not foster despair but can promote a most profound appreciation for life's possibilities.

Leo Tolstoy once said that people have not begun to think until they have addressed this question: "Is there any meaning in my life that the inevitable death awaiting me does not destroy?" [17, p. 24]. The answers will be as diverse as the people who contemplate the question. The heart of the question is not why we must die but how should we live.

Many believe that the answer to that question is to be found in religion. Politicians often say the United States was founded on Judeo-Christian values, others say our values come from the ideas of Enlightenment philosophers. Although Western European Christianity has influenced the moral and intellectual development of the United States, Judeo-Christian values have not been fully implemented. This does not negate the Bible as a place of understanding. It is worth reading and studying for its wisdom, whether one is a Christian or not.

One of the most important values in Christianity is forgiveness, but it is hard to find forgiveness in the customs and institutional practices of our society. A brief survey of courtrooms across the country will disabuse anyone of such a notion, and the survey does not have to be restricted to those highly publicized cases like the woman who sued McDonald's because she spilled their coffee on her lap. There was a court case which resulted in the jury awarding $10 to the plaintiff and scolding all parties involved for not resolving the problem out of court. When people do wrong we put them in prison, and we complain if the prisons are too nice or if the prisoners are released too soon. And we build more prisons.

Instead of forgiving, Americans want to punish those who make mistakes or who disagree with us. We ignore the criteria given as the basis for the Last Judgment. Sitting in judgment of the souls which come before him, Jesus welcomes one group into heaven because:

> I was hungry and you gave me food, I was thirsty and you gave me drink, I was a stranger and you welcomed me, I was naked and you clothed me, I was sick and you visited me, I was in prison and you came to me [Matthew 23:35-36].

Another group is ordered to the eternal fire because they did not do these things. Those in both groups cannot remember having done or not done any of these things to Jesus himself, but he tells them:

> Truly, I say to you, as you did it to one of the least of these my brethren, you did it to me [Matthew 25:40].

Imagine the protests from the condemned souls. *Lord, we would have helped you if you needed help. We didn't help those others because they were wicked or vile or disgusting but we would never have turned our back on you. They were not worthy. They didn't deserve to be helped.* And here is how I imagine Christ's response, *Then you should have forgiven them their failure to be worthy and demonstrate that forgiveness by giving them the help they did not deserve.* Because Jesus emphasized forgiveness, it seems odd that he would condemn even these sinners rather than forgive them. It suggests that the only unforgivable sin is to refuse to forgive others.

For Christians, the criteria for salvation or condemnation described in the Last Judgment passage ought to be taken seriously since they surely believe that the fate of their eternal souls will be determined by it, but even for non-Christians the passage offers sound advice for an ethical evaluation of their behavior. This criteria may not appeal to everyone. To accept this criteria as an appropriate means of assessing one's life is to give a high priority to the values implicit in the behavior being advocated: altruism, benevolence, empathy, and forgiveness.

It is also important to note what this passage says about where judgment shall occur and who is to be the judge. The Bible is consistent about the issue of judgment starting in Genesis with Adam and Eve's expulsion from paradise for eating fruit from the tree of the Knowledge of Good and Evil. What did they do to deserve expulsion? According to the serpent, eating the fruit of the tree would make them "like God." They believed the serpent and ate the fruit. The first consequence of this act was to recognize and be ashamed of their naked bodies. The result of the original sin of disobedience was to pass judgment on themselves, believing their understanding of good and evil to be equivalent to God's. Making such judgments meant that they had taken a responsibility that belonged only to God, a point made not only in passages from the Hebrew Scriptures but in the New Testament as well:

> Judge not, that you be not judged. For with the judgment you pronounce you will be judged, and the measure you give will be the measure you get [Matthew 7:1-2].

There are many passages in the Bible which unequivocally proclaim God as the appropriate authority for making judgments of others while admonishing humankind to refrain from passing judgment and to forgive one another. People who judge others in the name of God, citing the Bible as the basis of judgment, betray the human desire to play God by usurping God's role. When we judge others we are taking the well worn path; we are following on serpent trails on sacred ground. We are apple eating again.

To be forgiving is take the road less traveled, especially when another is harming you. Peter put the issue bluntly, "Lord, how often shall my brother sin against me, and I forgive him? as many as seven times?" Anyone who has read the gospels knows how to interpret Peter's question. Responding with forgiveness seven times seems more than generous to Peter, and on the eighth transgression Peter wants to wreak some righteous wrath on his brother. He might even *smite* his brother, but only with Christ's blessing. Jesus disappoints Peter by refusing to justify punishment. Instead Peter is told to forgive "seventy times seven," and immediately after saying this Jesus tells the parable of the unforgiving servant which vividly illustrates why we must forgive the sins of others if we want God to forgive our sins.

The servant was about to be sold, along with his wife and children, to pay the debt he owed his master. The man pleaded with his master for patience and promised to pay his debt as soon as possible. The master had compassion and forgave the debt. As he left his master's house, the servant saw a man who owed him money, confronted the man and demanded payment. This man admitted he could not pay his debt, but as the servant had done with his master, he pleaded for patience and promised to pay as soon as possible. The servant showed no mercy but promptly called the authorities and had the man arrested. Hearing of this, the master ordered the servant brought back before him. The master chastised the servant for not offering the same compassion that had been given to him. The master then rescinded his previous decision regarding this servant's debt and "delivered him to the tormentors." Unlike other parables, there is little ambiguity here. To eliminate any doubt, Jesus concludes, "So also my heavenly Father will do to every one of you, if you do not forgive your brother from your heart" [Matthew 18:21-35].

This parable and the last judgment passage offer good advice for people of all faiths and for those who believe in none. We can measure the quality of our lives by how we respond to the needs of the lost, the lonely, the most vulnerable members of our human family. Every aging elder in a nursing home is kin to us. We should show the same compassion we want to be shown as we age and weaken and become ever more vulnerable. The child brutalized by poverty is part of our extended family. We should nurture that child as we want our own children nurtured. If we forgive others and treat them well, we make our community a better place. If we disregard, disparage, or damage others, we nurture a brutality that may someday destroy its creators. Is it idealistic to talk of making the world a better place? Of course. That's why we must attempt it.

The joy of living is not to be found in the achievements but in the struggle to achieve. The great adventure of life is the journey, not the destination, and the adventure ends at the grave. The wisdom of the last judgment passage is also a challenge to live without rancor or regret, to respond to the needs of others, to seek and offer forgiveness, to love life. We should care about others because they are part of our adventure; they are sharing the journey with us.

To stay on the path in a dark and wayward world, we must let forgiveness lead and keep despair behind. If we stumble upon a place where we experience the wonder of life or the mystery of love, in that moment we will know the joy of the journey. Each time we discover such a place, we suspect there is something more at the end than rotting flesh and crumbling bones. Although no one knows for certain, Walt Whitman suggests a possibility:

> And to die is different from what anyone supposed, and luckier [18, p. 27].

# CHAPTER SEVEN
## In the Key of G:  GRACE

### THREE QUESTIONS

A King became convinced that if he could know the answers to three questions, he would never fail in anything he attempted. The questions were: How can I learn to do the right thing at the right time? Who are the people I need most and should pay the most attention to? What affairs are the most important and need my first attention? Having asked the wise men in his kingdom, who gave no satisfactory answer, the King sought a hermit of legendary wisdom who lived deep in the wood. Since the hermit received only common folk, the King put on simple clothes, left his horse and bodyguard far from the hermit's cottage, and walked alone.

The King found the hermit digging in his garden and asked his three questions, but the hermit merely kept digging. Since the old man appeared frail and weak, the King offered to turn over the dirt for him and the hermit accepted his offer. Hours passed and each time the King looked to see if the hermit was ready to respond, the hermit only offered to take the spade which the King refused to give him. Finally it was getting late in the day and the King was beginning to lose hope when a bearded man came running from the wood, blood flowing from his stomach. The King carried the man to the hermit's cottage and washed and bandaged the wound as best as he could. Since the blood continued lo flow, the King continued to rebandage the wound until the bleeding stopped. By now the sun had set and the King was so tired from the strenuous day's work that he lay down on the dirt floor and fell asleep.

When the King awoke in the morning the bearded man was staring at him. "Forgive me," said the bearded man in a weak voice. The King was startled but the man continued. "You don't know me, but I swore to revenge myself on you because you executed my brother and seized his property. I heard that you were going to visit the hermit so I followed you and hid myself in the wood along the path you would take to return and there I planned to kill you. When the day passed and you still had not returned, I decided to go after you, but your bodyguards spotted me and attacked me. Although they wounded me I managed to get away, but I would have bled to death if you had not taken care of my wounds. You have saved my life. If you wish, I will serve you as your most faithful slave and will bid my sons do the same!" The King not only forgave him but said he would ask his own physician to attend him and he would restore his property to him.

Preparing to leave, the King confronted the hermit one last time with his three questions and this time the hermit replied:

> Do you not see? Yesterday you pitied my weakness and dug these beds for me. If you had not and instead gone on your way that man would have attacked you. So the most important time was when you were digging for me and I was the most important person and to do me good was your most important business. When that man ran to us, the most important time was when you were attending to him otherwise he would have died and not made peace with you. He was the most important man and what you did for him was the most important business. Remember: there is only one time that is important—Now! It is the most important time because it is the only time when we have any power. The most necessary man is he with whom you are, for no man knows whether he will ever have dealings with anyone else, and the most important affair is to do him good, because for that purpose alone was man sent into this life [1].

---

**Grace**—the quality of being considerate and thoughtful, having moral strength . . . a virtue or excellence of divine origin (the spirit of God operating in man) . . . the freely given and unmerited favor and love of God.

---

Grace concludes my list of values, and I begin by describing what it means to be "grace-full." This is not intended to describe a person who moves with admirable coordination and skill but rather a person filled with grace. This is not the same as a gracious person, for such a person could also be condescending and thus not grace-full.

Grace is a concept that originated in Christian thought, but one does not have to be a Christian to appreciate it. To have grace is to be blessed and to know it. Grace includes self-love and at the same time is self-effacing. To have grace is to feel honored and yet undeserving of the honor. I once talked to a man who spoke enthusiastically about his wife; she was so wonderful he simply didn't deserve her. He was sincere. He didn't know what he had done to merit being loved by this amazing woman. When he talked about her his smile brought a joyful glow to his face, betrayed only by his verbal bewilderment at the mystery of her love. He was both proud and humble, but distinctly grateful. In those few moments when he described his wife, he exemplified what it means to be filled with grace.

The Christian meaning of grace is analogous. Christians believe God loves them even though they haven't earned such love, could never do enough to earn such love, and do not deserve such love; even so, it is a gift from God, freely given. The Christian concept of grace includes both humility and gratitude, an awareness of being incomplete, unfulfilled, but a human being whose worth is affirmed by the love of God—having a life made worthy by that love.

Being a Christian offers one way to find grace but not the only way. Another way is to confront your own mortality. Most people don't like to think about death, and may spend a substantial amount of time in activities to escape from the routine of daily life. It has been argued that the most powerful appeal of religion is in the answers it offers to the ultimate question: "What will happen to me after I die?" At times I have wondered how many Christians would maintain their faith and live by its principles if it did not include a belief in a soul that survives the demise of the body. One could ask the same question of Muslims or other faiths which promise immortality to all true believers.

Confronting mortality means to peer into the abyss and confront the darkness, the mystery, acknowledging that we can never know what follows death, if anything. Such an acknowledgment allows us to look at life with a greater appreciation for the privilege of being alive, and it can transform our perceptions of ourselves and others. An awareness of death can foster both sorrow and joy because when others suffer it diminishes our joy in being alive. Such suffering should be the catalyst for our compassion for all those made miserable by poverty, poor health, war, or the various misfortunes that afflict human beings.

To have grace is to understand that life is a gift, a gift that was not earned, is not deserved, but has been given nonetheless. One can only be humble in expressing appreciation for the gift, yet glad to have received it. With this gift comes the responsibility of using it wisely. I have been given this life. What shall I do with it? How can my actions express my gratitude for the privilege of being alive for whatever length of time I will have?

I knew an elementary school principal who would walk the school hallways and periodically slip into a classroom for a few minutes to see what the teacher and students were doing. Before he left he would often look at the students with a huge smile and say with great sincerity, "Isn't this great? Isn't this fun?" The students knew it wasn't a question but an assertion. This was his truth, and he believed it and lived it. For him, every day in school was a day of joy. His grace-fullness was apparent in his enthusiastic regard for learning.

---

**Pride**—a reasonable or justifiable self-respect . . . an exaggerated opinion of one's importance . . . a feeling of self-esteem arising from one's accomplishments, possessions . . . an inordinate self-esteem . . . a favorable idea of one's own appearance, achievements, or advantages . . . arrogant behavior or conduct.

---

Pride contrasts with grace. Parents and teachers tell children to "be proud of who you are" and "take pride in your accomplishments" to foster the child's self-esteem. It is important for children to believe in themselves and their abilities, but pride can slip beyond control. Without a counter-balance, *justifiable self-respect* becomes exaggerated beyond justification; a healthy self-esteem can become an *inordinate self-esteem*. Most of us have met the grace-less kind of person who owes nothing to anyone and is solely responsible for his or her success.

Grace permits pride in one's achievements, but an awareness of death provides balance. To be conscious of mortality is to be constantly reminded of the transitory nature of achievements. Writers whose books were immensely popular in their lifetime are no longer in print whereas artists who died in poverty and obscurity have works in prestigious museums. Most people will not have a lasting impact on the world even if they achieve fame and fortune, for fame and fortune are also transitory. Some of the wealthiest of the English aristocracy are buried in Westminster Abbey, but few people can read the epitaphs on their tombs because they are in Latin. Latin was the universal language in their day and the obvious choice for a monument to preserve their names for posterity, but English, which was their native tongue, is more likely to be understood by the people from all over the world who visit the Abbey today.

Wealth does not assure immortality. Fame does not assure immortality. Only a handful of human beings will be remembered for their accomplishments long after their death; therefore it is absurd to take excessive pride in one's accomplishments. The grace-full person realizes this. The grace-full person understands that what is important is to have a passion for a career or cause that contributes to the human community. The pursuit of that passion creates a sense of purposefulness during one's lifetime.

To be aware of one's own finite existence is to be aware of the mortality of others. Some die young, so young, before they have finished with childhood. Such deaths can cause some to ask "Why them and not me?" They surely loved life, and they may have had talents greater than mine, might have contributed more to humanity. It is difficult for pride in one's achievements to become arrogance in the humbling light of such honest considerations. As John Donne said, "never send to know for whom the bell tolls" because each person's death "diminishes me" [2, pp. 440-441].

Grace derives from the Latin word for gratitude which also spawned "grazie," the Italian word for *thank you*. A grace-full person approaches life with this sense of thanks-giving, appreciating the gift of life as well as the others engaged in the journey. The King in Tolstoy's tale has experienced a moment of grace. He saved the life of an enemy and gained a friend. The hermit tells the King what he must do to have such moments of grace in the future. Tolstoy does not tell us if the King heeded the hermit's message. Each of us makes a life in context with others. As they make their contributions to our life experience, so should we contribute to theirs in gratitude for what they have given us. At the end of life there will be nothing left but to face death with the kind of hope and prayer attributed to a soldier just before he fought in the battle of Blenheim:

O God, if there be a God, save my soul, if I have a soul! [3, p. 28]

ε❧  ε❧  ε❧

## HEARING VOICES

*For we are all strangers before thee, and sojourners, as were all our fathers: our days on the earth are as a shadow, and there is none abiding.*
First Chronicles (29:15)

*And thou wilt give thyself relief, if thou doest every act of thy life as if it were the last.*
Marcus Aurelius

*Old or young, we are all on our last
cruise.*
>                    Robert Louis Stevenson

> *Men talk of killing time, while time
> quietly kills them.*
>>                    Dion Boucicault

*Resolved, never to do anything which
I should despise or think meanly of in
another. Resolved, never to do anything
out of revenge. Resolved, never to do
anything which I should be afraid to
do if it were the last hour of my life.*
>                    Jonathan Edwards

> *Whatsoever thy hand findeth to do, do it
> with thy might; for there is no work, nor
> device, nor knowledge, nor wisdom, in
> the grave, whither thou goest.*
>>                    Ecclesiastes (9:10)

*Believe each day that has dawned is
your last.*
>                    Horace

> *All men think all men are mortal, but
> themselves.*
>>                    Edward Young

*Two men look out through the same bars:
One sees the mud, and one the stars.*
>                    Frederick Langbridge

> *The eternal silence of these infinite
> spaces (the stars) terrifies me.*
>>                    Blaise Pascal

*Ah, what a dusty answer gets the soul
When hot for certainties in this our life!*
>                    George Meredith

> *Books explain life.*
>>                    Gotthold Ephraim Lessing

*The person who does not read good
books has no advantage over the
person who can't read them.*
Mark Twain

*Faith is the substance of things hoped
for, the evidence of things not seen.*
Hebrews (11:1)

*There lives more faith in honest doubt,
Believe me, than in half the creeds.*
Alfred, Lord Tennyson

*Hope is a light diet, but very stimulating.*
Honore de Balzac

*To travel hopefully is a better thing
than to arrive, and the true success
is to labour.*
Robert Louis Stevenson

*Death never takes the wise man by
surprise; he is always ready to go.*
Jean de La Fontaine

*And almost everyone when age,
Disease, or sorrows strike him,
Inclines to think there is a God,
Or something very like Him.*
Arthur Hugh Clough

*Everyone who is without passion has
within no principles of action, nor motive
to act.*
Claude Adrien Helvetius

*Only the actions of the just
Smell sweet, and blossom in their dust.*
James Shirley

*I do not want the peace which passeth
understanding, I want the understanding
which bringeth peace.*
Helen Keller

## THERE BUT FOR THE GRACE OF GOD

I met Clifford Zepf in eighth grade. Clifford had some kind of disability that restricted his mobility. Occasionally I would see him riding around town in his specially built tricycle with the wire basket between the two rear wheels. Clifford was in several of my classes, but I never talked to him. No one at my school was cruel to Clifford, not even the bullies. We merely acted as though he didn't exist, which was perhaps even more cruel. If anyone thought about him at all it was probably to pity him, in the words of the old cliche, "there but for the grace of God go I." The new high school was completed by the time we were sophomores so Clifford did not attend class any more. He would eavesdrop on classes by means of a special communication system connecting classrooms in the school to his home. He could not say anything to us, but he could listen to what we said. Apparently Clifford completed all the homework and passed all the tests because his name was included with the rest of my graduating class. He did not attend the graduation ceremony.

I was reminded of Clifford Zepf during my first year as a high school teacher when I was told that one of my students was diagnosed as mentally retarded. Mainstreaming was not mandated yet so there were only a few students with some kind of disability in school and those few had only mild to moderate disabilities. Students with disabilities as severe as Clifford's were usually sent to special schools. I was teaching in college by the time the law was passed which mandated that public schools include students with disabilities in regular classrooms. I was glad to see this law enacted because I remembered Clifford Zepf. Clifford probably had much to offer his classmates, but we will never know. We treated him as if his disability was contagious and kept our distance. The teachers did nothing to help Clifford's peers view him as a person. His disability was all we saw and all we knew of him.

I had a similar experience during my senior year in college. I was visiting my older sister in Iowa when her husband asked me if I wanted to come with him. He was going to visit a student from one of his classes at the community college. He said she was intelligent, loved reading literature, and that I would enjoy talking to her. David had just called to make sure she was home and to ask if he could come over to return her paper. I went with him.

On the way to her house, David talked enthusiastically about Anita's writing. He described her not only as a thoughtful person but a good writer. The paper she had just written for him was the best he had ever read in his many years of teaching. As we parked in front of the two story white frame house, David explained that this was her parents' home, but a few years ago they had added a room onto the back of the house built especially for their daughter.

Anita had severe cerebral palsy. She needed a wheelchair when she left the house, but her room had been constructed with a ledge six inches high around the perimeter of the room on which she kept everything she needed. David described how she could drag herself across the floor to move around the room. This was not easy for her, but she preferred getting around in this fashion to sitting in a wheelchair all the time.

This brief explanation was given as David and I walked up to the house. David knocked on the door and a voice told us to come in. I looked around as we walked into the room and it was just as David had described it. The floor was carpeted and free of obstructions, the wooden ledge that went around the room was about two feet wide. In addition to practical items such as books, pens, notebooks, and an old typewriter, there were also some decorative items such as a statue of Michelangelo's David, a German beer stein, and a few framed black and white photographs.

What David had not described was Anita herself, so I was unprepared for what I saw when we entered her room. I was shocked by her obesity. At first I could not imagine how her arms were strong enough to pull that large body across the carpet. As I watched her move around I realized that only her upper body was large. Her hips were small and you could tell her legs were thin and withered despite being concealed in sweat pants. Her dark hair was cropped short and its blackness contrasted with the pasty white pallor of her face. Her chin was small but her lips were large and her nose tilted upward so far that even though she was sitting on the floor you could see her nostrils. She reminded me of Victor Hugo's description of Quasimodo, and like his malformed creation, she could have won a prize for ugliness.

We stayed at her home quite a while, almost an hour as I recall. David and Anita did almost all of the talking. I simply stared at Anita as if she were my private freak show and I was trying to get my money's worth. I was especially interested in watching her drag herself around the room. She was actually quite good at it and managed to move about efficiently despite her bulky body. She wasn't quick, but she was persistent and determined. At last David said we had to leave. I said, "Nice to have met you," and she thanked me for coming.

David continued talking about the issues he and Anita had just been discussing until we got in the car. David put his keys in the ignition, then turned to me and said, "So, what did you think of her?" I hesitated as I tried to think of something to say and finally said something about her being "interesting." David nodded and started the car. At that moment I realized that I could not remember one word Anita had said in almost an hour of conversation. The fact that she was talking with David did not matter. With anyone else I would have paid attention to what was being said and formed an impression of the person speaking, but this time I did not. I had been so obsessed by her physical appearance that this was all I could recall. I had learned nothing about her, her ideas, her love of literature or anything else David talked about. I did not know any more about her than I had known about Clifford Zepf, and this time I could not use youth as my excuse. In another year I would be a teacher. My brother-in-law had not been so distracted by Anita's physical appearance that he could not relate to the person and the personality which defined her. I had become fixated on the form, and I was deeply ashamed.

Once again I had been given an opportunity to learn from someone whose experiences were different from mine, someone whose life had been shaped in ways I would never know. I had much to gain from Anita, but I had gained nothing. I wanted to tell David to turn the car around and go back, that I had made a mess of it and wanted to do it over, but I knew we could not do that. In the real world second chances are rare. You've got to get it right the first time.

As a high school teacher I never had a student like Anita in any class, but I did have a student who had problems because of his physical appearance. Karl had no disability, but he was odd looking. His head was too large for his short, thin body and to make matters worse he had a severe acne problem. Although old enough to drive a car, he rode a bicycle to school, not an expensive racing bike but an old, rusty, child-sized bike. Although I rarely saw him talking to other students, they talked to him, taunted him to be more precise. Several boys called him "zit face" and they would always ask if he washed his face today. Karl never responded to their cruel remarks. Girls would not say such things, but when Karl was around they would whisper to one another and roll their eyes and laugh.

Between classes and especially during lunch hour the students would often engage in a certain amount of teasing and good natured name calling, especially the boys. Teachers were not expected to intervene unless the tone of such comments became serious or hostile. Although there was no hostility in the name calling and comments Karl was subjected to, the words were certainly unkind, and because it happened every day it began to gnaw at me. One day when it was once again my turn to be the lunch room supervisor, I heard the predictable calls of "zit face" as Karl walked by a table of boys. I had had enough. I walked over to the boys to chastize them but then changed my mind. I wanted to talk to Karl first to ask if their insults bothered him and what he wanted me to do.

I walked past the boys and over to the table where Karl sat alone eating his lunch. As I sat down beside him I told him that I had heard what the boys said to him. I asked if he wanted me to talk to them and make them stop. He looked at me with a shy smile and said, "Oh it's all right. They're just teasing me. They don't mean anything by it." I wanted to tell him that this was more than teasing, but I had the sense to be quiet. Because he was painfully shy, Karl had little more to say, but it was obvious that he interpreted the boys' taunts as equivalent to the normal good natured banter they engaged in with each other. He used their cruelty to create the illusion that he was accepted, that he was one of them.

If the boys had not called Karl names they would have said nothing to him, and clearly that would have been worse for Karl. Despite having the best of intentions, I had almost interfered with this warped but symbiotic relationship. The boys made their derogatory comments to Karl to satisfy their need to feel superior to someone, and Karl transformed their comments into something that gave him a sense of belonging, of being part of his peer group. The relationship formed was not an attractive one, but it fulfilled its purpose for all parties involved.

Because of this incident, I began to think about how we misperceive problems. I was sure Karl had the problem and I wanted to help him get rid of it. By focusing on Karl I overlooked the real problem which was the boys' need to feel superior. Their need was a problem because it could only be satisfied at the expense of another, and their problem would not be solved by stopping the name calling. The solution would mean finding a way for adolescents to get beyond the superficial level of someone's physical appearance. Was it possible for them to recognize the person beneath Karl's acne scarred face? I could understand how someone could be distracted by a person's physical appearance, but this problem extended beyond physical deformities.

How do you get people to recognize that they have certain attitudes which degrade others based on factors such as a disability or race or being poor? Being aware of these attitudes is an essential first step, but then a person needs to understand how the attitudes developed and what can be done to eliminate them. I'm not certain of the best way to address this problem, and at times I worry that such problems cannot be fixed. It is hard to accept that.

During a summer festival at a riverside park, my wife and I were walking along the river enjoying the sun and the food and the music from the main stage. Between live performances, taped music was played over the loudspeakers on either side of the stage. A jazz band had just finished their set on the stage and I heard the familiar melody of "The Blue Danube." A short man walking toward me stopped and stared at the nearest loudspeaker. He smiled, lifted his arms above his head and began waving them in the air as if conducting an orchestra. I looked at him more closely. From his size and physical appearance, he seemed to be a dwarf; his facial features suggested that he might have Down Syndrome. I wondered if there was a particular reason why he took such pleasure in Strauss, but I shared his joy at hearing this music.

As I walked past the man I noticed a couple of boys, perhaps twelve or thirteen years old, staring at him. I hoped they wouldn't bother him, but as a teacher I knew how cruel boys of this age could be. As I kept walking, the thought of the boys doing something to spoil this man's pleasure nagged at me unceasingly until I finally turned around.

The two boys had been joined by a few more about the same age, and they stood around the short man as he continued smiling and waving his arms to the rhythms of the music. The boys whispered to each other; some laughed and pointed at the man, but he ignored them. More boys stopped and by now the man had attracted a small crowd. The boys no longer whispered but mocked the man with fake praise for his conducting performance. He must have heard them because he walked over to a wooden picnic table and crawled up on it. He wanted this higher ground so they could see him more clearly. With an unwavering smile, he resumed waving his arms. More boys joined the audience for this impromptu performance, gathering in a roughly oval shape as they crowded around the picnic table.

The teacher in me wanted to scold the boys and ask them if they had nothing better to do than make fun of a retarded man. I was tempted. It was hard to resist until I remembered Karl. When I asked myself what the problem was, I realized that it had nothing to do with the retarded man. He was still enjoying the music and perhaps even enjoying the attention of the small crowd gathered around him. I wanted to think that. I wanted to think that he refused to relinquish his pleasure in the music even though they mocked him and laughed at him.

My perception of the man seemed to be supported by the way he conducted himself as well as his invisible orchestra. He persisted in what he was doing with a pleasure far more genuine than the pleasure the boys were getting from their mockery. Their pleasure was fostered by an insecurity and an anxiety that would not allow them to display such a genuine feeling of joy. As the short man stood on the table, waving his arms, he demonstrated a kind of grace.

There was nothing I could do to solve the boys' problem. If it was ever to be solved it would happen as a result of age and maturity and hopefully the development of enough self-confidence to avoid such pathetic behavior, enough self-confidence so that even they, at some future time, could openly express a genuine feeling of joy for music or something else, anything. But not now. They could not possibly do that now. The boys could have gained much from observing this man if they could not only have seen his joy but shared it. All they could see was what seemed strange in him, and all they could do was laugh.

I have heard much talk about role models as if there is a select group of people whose actions are to be emulated, but there are lessons to be learned everywhere, and many may come from surprising sources. We were discussing mental retardation in a graduate class when one of my students said he had been a supervisor in a group home for men who had been identified as mentally retarded. He told of a time when the men had watched a beer commercial on television and talked about going downtown to a bar. The men became excited about this idea and they all wanted to go. The two supervisors discussed it and decided that there was no reason against it. After supper, all of the men climbed into the two vans and they were driven downtown.

When the bartender saw this group of men entering his bar, he seemed a bit uncomfortable, so one of the supervisors went over to explain. He assured the bartender that the supervisors from the group home would take responsibility for the men. The bartender gave everyone a beer and the men from the group home drank it and liked it. They ordered more. After a few beers the men were joking and laughing and a few were singing. They were having a good time and even the bartender seemed to enjoy them. When the supervisors felt it was time to leave, they told the men to finish their drinks so they could go home. They drove back to the group home and the supervisors made sure all the men got ready for bed and went to sleep.

The next morning, every one of the men woke up with a hangover. The supervisors realized that this offered what educators call a "teachable moment." After breakfast they called a group meeting to discuss the effects of alcohol. They said these unpleasant effects did not occur every time someone drank beer, but that nausea and headaches were the body's reaction to getting too much alcohol. These reactions were a possibility anytime a person consumed alcohol, so the men needed to understand that if they drank beer again they should be careful not to drink too much. The men talked about this, and they decided that the good time they had the previous night was not good enough to make up for the suffering they were enduring this morning. They took a vote on this issue and it was unanimous. "They voted never to drink again," the storyteller paused and looked around at the others, "and they never did." I smiled and said, "And we call *them* retarded?" Everyone laughed.

For six years I was on the Board of Directors for the Wisconsin Coalition for Advocacy, an agency which advocates for the rights of people with disabilities. I met people with different kinds of disabilities and I learned something from each of them. I am grateful for that. One of the lessons nearly every disabled person has learned from being disabled is to look past a person's physical appearance and accept others who might seem strange or different. This is a lesson we all need to learn. Another lesson I have learned from people with a disability is to live each day with a sense of wonder and gratitude. It is good to be alive. We often forget that. We will have a long time to experience being dead, if it is something that qualifies as an experience, but we only have this brief opportunity to enjoy life.

When I think back to my hometown and the perceptions people had of Clifford Zepf and others like him, it seems so strange now. To think or to say "there but for the grace of God go I" is to express pity for a person with an affliction and gratitude for not being so afflicted.

I have learned that having a disability is not necesssarily a sign of suffering but can signify a kind of grace. It is not automatic and it certainly is not genetic, but grace can be found in the hearts and minds of people who have learned to live with a disability. Such people have much to teach those of us who are nondisabled, if we are willing to pay attention, not like the boys in the park but like adults wise enough to look past the surface and into the soul. Good teachers come in all shapes and sizes and colors, and some of them come in wheelchairs. If we learn the lessons, we will be richly rewarded.

## ECHOES

*You don't get to choose how you're going to die. Or when. You can decide how you're going to live now.*
                                        Joan Baez

*Once you accept your own death . . . you are free to live. You no longer care about your reputation . . . except so far as you can be used to promote a cause you believe in.*

                                        Saul Alinsky

*You gain strength, courage and
confidence by every experience in
which you really stop to look fear in
the face . . . You must do the thing
which you think you cannot do.*

Eleanor Roosevelt

*Everything has been figured out except
how to live.*

Jean Paul Sartre

*Faith which does not doubt is dead faith.*

Miguel de Unamuno

*People say that life is the thing,
but I prefer reading.*

Logan Pearsall Smith

*The optimist proclaims that we live in
the best of all possible worlds; and the
pessimist fears this is true.*

James Branch Cabell

*The optimist is a better reformer than the
pessimist . . . The pessimist can be
enraged at evil, but only the optimist can
be surprised at it . . . It is not enough that
he should think injustice absurd . . . he
must have the faculty of a violent and
virgin astonishment.*

G. K. Chesterton

*Idealists . . . foolish enough to throw
caution to the winds . . . have advanced
humanity and have enriched the world.*

Emma Goldman

*Two roads diverged in a wood, and I,
I took the one less traveled by,
And that has made all the difference.*

Robert Frost

*If you do not tell the truth about yourself
you cannot tell it about other people.*

Virginia Woolf

*The truth comes as a conqueror because we have lost the art of receiving it as a guest.*

Rabindranath Tagore

*The opposite of a correct statement is a false statement, but the opposite of a profound truth may well be another profound truth.*

Niels Bohr

*I do not believe that sheer suffering teaches. If suffering alone taught, all the world would be wise since everyone suffers. To suffering must be added mourning, understanding, patience, love, openness and the willingness to remain vulnerable.*

Anne Morrow Lindbergh

*Man is born broken. He lives by mending. The grace of God is glue.*

Eugene O'Neill

*As life is action and passion, it is required of an individual that he should share the passion and action of his time, at peril of being judged not to have lived.*

Oliver Wendell Holmes, Jr.

*Set me a task in which I can put something of my very self, and it is a task no longer; it is joy; it is art.*

Bliss Carmen

*Life is change. Growth is optional. Choose wisely.*

Karen Kaiser Clark

*We are all in the gutter, but some of us are looking at the stars.*

Oscar Wilde

## SEARCHING FOR SONGLINES

> Aboriginal people believe in what they call a songline that runs right down through the center of Australia and each section of the line is a verse and at the end of each verse is a sacred site like a station on a railway line and they feel the song as they walk along the line, and they can run faster when they're on the line, in tune, and they slow down and become stupid when they veer off course.
>
> Paul Cox

Ever since I learned about the songlines of Australian aborigines I have thought of them as a metaphor for values. Like the songlines, the most deeply held values should guide us to sacred sites where we can appreciate the experience of life. In such a place a person may suddenly feel a sense of connectedness with nature, with humanity, with God, or with *everythingatonce*. When we say we believe in a particular value but we behave inconsistently with regard to that value, we veer off course and behave stupidly as described above in the excerpt from the screenplay of the movie "Cactus," written and directed by Australian filmmaker Paul Cox.

I have been an avid reader since I was seven years old, probably because I have always found passages that moved me, that presented me with a way of seeing or feeling or thinking that I found compelling. One of the earliest books that affected me was a novel called *Beautiful Joe* by Marshall Saunders [4]. I read it four times when I was a child. As an adult I read the book to my children and was surprised to discover it was primarily a sentimental story of a boy and his dog, but the opening chapter reminded me of why the book had moved me as a child.

A dog belonging to a drunk has just had a litter. The owner was a cruel man, especially when drinking. Suffering from a hangover early one morning, he stumbles upon the litter who scatter in response to his roaring curses. He manages to snatch one unlucky pup and takes him to the chopping block where the man chops off its ears and tail. A newspaper boy hears the howling and investigates. Seeing the bleeding pup and the bloody hatchet, he attacks the man who drops the wounded animal. The boy wraps the whimpering puppy in a newspaper and takes him home. As the wounds heal, the boy considers a name for his new pet. Realizing how ugly the mutilated animal will appear to others, the boy calls him Beautiful Joe, so that every time he is called the dog will hear a name that defies the mutilation done to his body and defines him as something finer than what his appearance might suggest.

Rescuing the dog from a vicious master was a conventional act of kindness consistent with other adventures in the novel, but the name given to the dog illustrates how kindness can offer a moment of grace.

Moments of grace are moments of transcendence. Moments where people see beyond the limitations of conventional reality to a larger, grander vision. Such moments are not always dramatic. When comedian Dick Gregory was asked why he called his autobiography *Nigger,* he said it was so that every time a white person used that epithet it would advertise his book. Gregory shows us how humor can be used to transcend personal pain and anger. It is an achievement made possible by grace.

In reading books I am looking and hoping for such moments as if searching for songlines, as if I were stranded on the Outback looking for signposts to steer me in the right direction. I want to find songlines which will guide me to a better understanding of others. I am looking for paths which allow me to pursue a deeper appreciation of life from those who lived before or who share the journey with me now. I want to know what others have learned on the pathways they have traveled and what I can learn from them. I am searching for songlines which will lead me to a moment of grace, a sacred site.

I first read Saki's short story "The Interlopers" [5] when I was in high school. As a storm approaches, two men from feuding families are prowling on their disputed forest land. With guns in hand they stumble upon each other and are momentarily startled. Before either can fire his weapon, the storm fells a tree pinning the men beneath it. Initially both men curse one another and each prays for his men to come first, not only to be rescued but to kill the other. As time passes the two men become aware of each other's pain, and each feels sympathy for the other man's suffering. The hatred in their hearts fades as they are forced to face their human frailty. By the end each prays for his men to come first to have the honor of rescuing the other. They hear sounds of someone coming and hope their ordeal is over until one of them recognizes the sound and begins to laugh, not in relief but in despair. When the other asks what's wrong, the answer is given in one word: *"Wolves."*

Developing a concern for others can lead to moments of grace, but Saki's story includes a warning: do not assume you will always have time to atone for the wrongs you may have done. There are no guarantees. This was something I told my son. Jason was six years old when his sister was born. After an initial period of harmony he started teasing Tess. Often he would not stop until she was so angry she was screaming or in tears. As the older brother, Jason was primarily responsible for determining the kind of relationship he and Tess would have. He chose sibling rivalry. When he spoke to her it was almost always to tease or taunt or criticize her. On many occasions I told him how much better it would be for the entire family if he would have a more positive relationship with Tess, and I frequently reminded him that he had the power to change the relationship anytime. He did not choose to change it.

By the time Jason was a freshman in college, he seemed to be interested in such a change. During visits home he gave the impression of a boy becoming a man, not merely growing older but becoming more mature. He was willing to be the big brother who could be trusted as a confidante and would give good advice, but ten years of tormenting Tess stood between them. It would take time for her to trust him. Jason had just begun his sophomore year when he was killed in a car accident. He had not created many good memories for his sister to treasure in his absence. Now it was too late.

Tess and I have talked about Jason. I have shared my memories in words and in writing, but it's not the same as having good memories of her own. The best advice I can give her is based on a comment by Holden Caulfield at the end of J. D. Salinger's *Catcher in the Rye*. Throughout the book Holden has been recalling all the people he has met as he talks to a psychoanalyst, and these memories provide Holden with an insight which becomes a moment of grace. Many of the people he described were not admirable and his experiences with them were not enjoyable, but in remembering them Holden realizes that the story of his life has been formed with them: "About all I know is, I sort of *miss* everybody I told about" [6, p. 214]. Life is a collaborative experience. The people we meet may cause us pain or give us joy. Good or bad, the experiences we have become the journey that shapes who we are. No matter how Jason treated Tess, he is still part of her. This is how she should remember him, and I hope she misses him.

Movies represent another source of songlines. One of my favorite examples is a scene from the film "Gandhi," which won the Academy Award for Best Picture in 1982. In response to an outbreak of violence between Hindus and Muslims, Gandhi says he will fast until the fighting stops. At first he is ignored, but as he continues to fast he becomes weaker and many fear he will die before the fighting in the streets stops. As Gandhi lies in bed, a Hindu man approaches him and throws a package onto the bed. He is immediately seized by Gandhi's bodyguards who check the package—it is simply food. The man demands that Gandhi eat. He says that Muslims killed his ten-year-old son and he has killed Muslims in revenge. He knows his soul is lost because he has taken lives so he will keep killing Muslims, but he does not want the death of such a great soul as Gandhi's on his conscience. He insists that Gandhi eat the food.

Gandhi says the man's soul is not lost forever. There is a way for the man to redeem his soul if he will listen carefully and do exactly what Gandhi tells him. The man calms down and listens. Gandhi says there are many children living on the streets now because their parents have been killed as a consequence of the recent violence. He tells the man to search for such a child, find one that is about the age of his son and take him home. The man must take care of this child and raise him as his son. Gandhi pauses, then says there is one more thing the man must do: "You must raise the child as a Muslim."

This songline shows how empathy can take us to a moment of grace, and why it is a sacred place. Abraham Lincoln understood this, and he responded to such moments with humility. During one official reception, Lincoln said he regarded all Southerners simply as erring human beings rather than hated foes. A woman who was proud of being a staunch Unionist criticized him for speaking kindly of the enemy when he should have been speaking of their destruction. "Madam," Lincoln said, "do I not destroy my enemies when I make them my friends?" [7, p. 53].

It is easy to hate, a fact documented to excess in human history, it is far more difficult to be concerned for others, to worry about their well-being, to forgive them their faults. Even so, the songlines have been given for us to follow if we are willing to listen and learn. Mark Twain offers a refrain in *The Adventures of Huckleberry Finn*. Amidst the humor, satire, and social commentary, Huck is forced to resolve an especially troubling dilemma. He accepts society's definition of a slave as property, so helping Jim escape from Miss Watson means he is stealing her property in clear violation of the law and the Ten Commandments. He is placing both body and soul in peril. Huck finally decides to do the right thing according to these social standards: he writes a letter to Miss Watson to let her know where she can find Jim.

Writing the letter makes Huck feel "washed clean of sin for the first time . . . in my life," but as he recalls his recent adventures, he remembers Jim's many acts of kindness toward him, and he remembers how Jim has worried about Huck and how they have helped one another. Huck remembers telling Jim that he was Jim's best friend. Huck looks at his letter to Miss Watson:

> I was a trembling, because I'd got to decide forever, betwixt two things, and I knowed it. I studied a minute, sort of holding my breath, and then says to myself: "All right, I'll go to Hell"—and tore it up [8, p. 180].

Huck's decision flies in the face of everything his Judeo-Christian society has told him, but this act of wickedness permits him to transcend that reality. The color of a person's skin should not diminish their humanity, and differences should not be used as an excuse to condemn another to a life of misery. Huck has learned a lesson about diversity and it is for him a moment of grace.

There are many songlines in the Bible, but the story of an adulterous woman may be one of the best examples of grace [9]. Teachers of the law bring a woman before Jesus who has not only committed the sin of adultery, but she was caught "in the act." Her guilt is not based on rumor or hearsay. The woman is indisputably a sinner and the law demands death as the punishment for this sin. The teachers of the law have brought the woman to Jesus to hear how he will adjudicate the matter, to see how he will maintain his message of forgiveness without violating the laws. They challenge him, "Now Moses in the law commanded us, that such should be stoned: but what sayest thou?"

Advising these men to stone the woman would contradict his message of forgiveness, but insisting that they forgive her and refrain from stoning her would make Jesus guilty of contradicting Mosaic law. He does neither. Instead he tells them how to select individuals who could claim the moral right to take this woman's life: only those who have never sinned could justify taking the life of this woman because she has sinned. The accusers recognize the wisdom of his words and, knowing their own sins, they walk away.

After those who had accused the woman leave, Jesus is the only one left to pass judgment on her. Instead of passing judgment, he asks her a question, "Hath no man condemned thee?" The woman responds, "No man, Lord." Was there no person who could meet Jesus' criteria, no one free of sin who therefore had the right to stone to death the adulterous woman? Based on conventional Christian beliefs, Jesus would be the only person who would qualify. To carry out the wisdom of His own statement about who was qualified to take a life, Jesus should become the woman's executioner. Instead Jesus says, "Neither do I condemn thee."

When I hear Christian fundamentalists talk about Jesus, it often seems as though they are not talking about a forgiving Christ but a righteous Messiah who would feel justified in stoning this woman to death. Struggling to be reconciled with this Christ who seems almost too kind, too forgiving, some Christians prefer to emphasize the comment Jesus makes before sending the woman away, "Go, and sin no more." They offer this as proof that Jesus disapproved of sinful behavior, but what else was Jesus supposed to say, "Have a nice day?" He is giving her good advice: live a virtuous life. What if she did not take that advice? What would Jesus have said if the adulterous woman had sinned again? If we take Him at His word, He would have forgiven her again, "seventy times seven."

This story is a compelling illustration of the principle that people need to recognize their own flaws and forgive others as they would want to be forgiven. This story illustrates the wisdom of forgiveness. Its message is that even when we are justified in our desire to punish another, even if that person richly deserves to be punished, we should still forgive them. This is a message that transcends human wisdom, it offers us a vision of grace.

One of the most remarkable stories I have ever read combines all of the songlines creating harmony in the human community, and it is not fiction. It is the story of C. P. Ellis from North Carolina who was once the "exalted cyclops" for the Durham chapter of the Ku Klux Klan. The factors that lead Ellis to his hatred were common to those who join the Klan: his father had been a Klansman; he was not well educated; he was poor. He needed someone to blame so he blamed Black people, especially Ann Atwater, a Civil Rights leader in Durham. Ellis did not disguise his hate for Black people but attended public meetings to express it. When the school board met to discuss school desegregation, Ellis was there. When the city council was confronted by Civil Rights activists, Ellis was there. He was being privately praised by many highly respectable members of those governance bodies but never in person, only late at night over the telephone. Ellis wondered why they avoided him in public.

In an attempt to resolve the school desegregation conflict, Ellis and Atwater were named as the co-chairs of a committee to explore options and come up with recommendations. Although they "had cussed each other" and hated each other, they did not know each other. As they tried to find common ground on the issue, they discovered their common ground as human beings. At one meeting Atwater began to weep, then explained that her children were being taunted in school. The same thing was happening to Ellis's children, and he stumbled into a moment of grace:

> . . . here we are, two people from the far ends of the fence, havin' iden-
> tical problems, except hers bein' black and me bein' white. From that
> moment on, that gal and I worked together good. I begin to love the
> girl, really. (He weeps.) [10, p. 229].

Ellis uses this moment to transform his life. He understands that respectable people have shunned him in public because it would embar-rass them to be seen with him, and that poor whites have more in common with poor Blacks than with wealthy whites who manipulate them. A moment of empathy creates the possibility for Ellis to learn the value of diversity. He begins collaborating with Atwater on Civil Rights issues. He goes back to school to finish his high school diploma. Because of his concern for workers he becomes a Union organizer.

Ellis remembers his past with shame. He recalls rejoicing when Martin Luther King was assassinated, but when he listens to King's speeches now, tears come to his eyes. He knows he must forgive himself and he is committed to doing good and helping others:

> The whole world was openin' up and I was learnin' new truths . . . it was almost like bein' born again. It was a new life. I didn't have these sleepless nights I used to have when I was active in the Klan . . . I could sleep at night and feel good about it [10, p. 230].

This story asks us to believe that an ordinary man can make an extraordinary transformation to a life filled with compassion and commitment and grace.

What makes such transformations possible? When my daughter was six years old her Fisher Price toy castle was one of her favorite playthings. One day I noticed that she had left the drawbridge down and had written WELCOME on it with a crayon. I smiled at the contradiction, but then it began to seem like a useful metaphor. All people build walls to protect themselves from others, as a defense against unexpected attacks. These are substantive barriers which can't be whisked away by a magician's sleight of hand. We must begin by opening ourselves up, by letting the drawbridge down. This will require taking risks: being open to new experiences, helping those who need help, welcoming others into our lives, learning from their strengths and forgiving their faults.

It sounds so deceptively simple, but none of this is easy. The starting point is the desire to travel to a sacred site, to value the transitory moment of grace it offers, and to believe that such moments can be used to build within us a more permanent state of grace. We must learn to sing the songlines that will take us to these sacred sites. It means to start, to get lost, to start again. It means learning from those who came before, searching for signposts in a strange land. It means expecting to fail while never failing to keep our expectations. It means believing we can hear the music of a songline, even if it is but the faintest echo in a gentle breeze.

Listen.

# Postlude

*If we are to build a stable cultural structure above that which threatens to engulf us by changing our lives more rapidly than we can adjust our habits, it will only be by flinging over the torrent a structure as taut and flexible as a spider's web, a human society deeply self-conscious and undeceived by the waters that race beneath it, a society more literate, more appreciative of human worth than any society that has previously existed. That is the sole prescription, not for survival—which is meaningless—but for a society worthy to survive.*

Loren Eiseley, *The Firmament of Time,* p. 147, Atheneum: New York, 1966.

# In Praise of Community

The values presented in this book are offered for consideration not simply in the spirit of self-improvement but in a communal spirit. Human beings are social beings. We do not live in isolation from others. We are part of communities, not only the city or town in which we live but the place where we work, the place where we worship, the organizations to which we belong. We live within and among a variety of communities, and that is a compelling reason for valuing community and embracing those values which strengthen community.

What does it mean to value community, to give community a high priority? It does not require an uncritical perception of your city or neighborhood. It does not necessarily mean joining a community organization to promote community welfare. People in such organizations have sometimes contradicted the meaning of community based on perceptions of self-interest. For example, a community organization was once formed for the explicit purpose of preventing an African-American family from purchasing a home in a segregated suburb. The organization ascribed lofty motives to their endeavor by calling themselves "The Good Neighbor Society," and by adopting the "Golden Rule" as their motto.

> **Community**—people with common interests living in a particular area or (with) a common government and common cultural and historical heritage . . . a unified body of interacting individuals in a particular location (from "commune"—to converse or talk together intimately . . . an interchange of ideas or sentiments).

The concept of community is founded on two key attributes—location and communication. It begins with people who settle or grow up in a particular place and stay there. When people live near each other they commune with one another. Their interaction leads to a knowledge of one another, relationships of a personal or commercial nature develop, common interests are identified and strengthened and a sense of unity evolves. Location alone provides the possibility for community, but communication creates community.

Today we live in an age of paradox with regard to communication. Because of the growth of the telecommunications industry, our ability to interact with others has expanded enormously. With television, telephone, FAX machines, and e-mail, communication is instantaneous and global. Yet someone living in an apartment complex with hundreds of other people may not know any of them intimately; someone living in a suburb may seldom talk to neighbors beyond a brief greeting if they happen to see one another. Because of the global media, especially television, people may know more about the lives of strangers in faraway places than they do about those who live next door.

We have even lost some symbols of community. A common architectural feature of homes in the United States used to be a front porch large enough to contain many chairs, perhaps a porch swing. Because such homes were usually built close to the street, the porches were open spaces symbolizing an open invitation to passersby. When people strolled down the street or sidewalk after supper, they might be invited to the porch for conversation and a cool drink on a warm summer evening, or a cup of cocoa to counter the crisp autumnal air. These front porches have almost disappeared today; many that remain have been enclosed. Modern designs eliminate them. We don't need front porches because we no longer commune with those who live next door. We commune with television, a distinctly one-sided conversation.

As our sense of community has declined, so has the value for community. To regain that value, the concept of community must be redefined. Attempts to resurrect the traditional idea of community can succeed on a small scale, but is likely to fail in a more ambitious effort because the traditional definition was based on a small scale: villages or towns or ethnic neighborhoods, places where everybody knew everybody else. Today we need to envision community on several levels, not just one's neighborhood, city, or state, but as a national and global enterprise. We need to recognize the bonds of humanity connecting us to those we see on our television screens. We need to understand their struggle for survival or to gain freedom from oppression. Only by supporting the freedom of others can we be assured of maintaining freedom for ourselves, and freedom has historically been an essential American value.

---

**Individuality**—a single human being as distinguished from a group . . . separate, especially from similar things . . . independence of thought or action; *Individualism* is the pursuit of individual rather than common or collective interests, also, the doctrine or belief that all actions are determined by or take place for the benefit of individuals, not the masses.

Some people claim that emphasizing the individual is the best way to foster freedom, but this is the approach we have taken in the United States, increasingly in recent years, and it has come at a cost to our sense of community. It may have promoted individual freedom but it has also promoted alienation and fear. We are all individuals, nothing can change that. We think our own thoughts, make our own choices, suffer our own consequences, but when the individual is celebrated as the highest priority, we make conflict inevitable and compromise unlikely. When the individual is held supreme, we force individuals to assert themselves and place their needs in competition with others. Helping others is motivated only by self-interest. Decisions are made to enhance personal interests at the expense of another, or many others.

If individual needs are defined as most important, and if what benefits an individual is perceived as the highest priority, how can conflicting interests be resolved? People will probably take as much as they could get without regard for the consequences to others. A focus on individuality destroys community because it produces a poisonous atmosphere of competing claims fostering suspicion and mistrust as people are polarized into haves and have nots. It is foolish to deny individuality because everyone wants to be recognized as a unique person, but we must find ways to celebrate that uniqueness and still have community.

Advocates for multicultural education believe that promoting pluralistic attitudes is a way to recognize individuality while creating community in a diverse society. Their critics contend that multiculturalism encourages a balkanization of America, but the fragmentation of our society has its roots in the perpetuation of a "them and us" mentality. Teaching students from multicultural perspectives challenges that mentality by providing students with information which includes all groups of people within the human family. We may be part of a particular group, but we are also part of humanity.

Most people belong to groups, both personal and professional. In these groups are the people we know best. We know their strengths and weaknesses. We make excuses for them when they behave badly and we celebrate their triumphs. We listen to them and try to understand their concerns and give them advice whether or not they want it because we feel connected to them and want them to succeed. We need to expand this attitude to the larger levels of community. We need to understand the problems and struggles of others outside of our most intimate groups and have a similar regard for their lives. We need to forgive their mistakes and celebrate their achievements. We need to listen and learn, and when we disagree, we need to accept compromise as the way to resolve our conflicts. This is what we must do if we want to create community within our society, and it is only in a society which has this kind of commitment to community that the individual has the freedom to flourish.

The idea of freedom being a consequence of giving community priority over the individual may seem like a paradox, but it is profoundly true. It is not a new idea, but it has been forgotten in our society. Community creates the context in which we live and learn, and that context has considerable importance for our ability to develop our individual talents and strengths. As we engage with others on common concerns, we promote a concept of community which benefits us as individuals. When we help solve the problems of others, we make it more likely that others will help us solve our own problems. To create community we must recognize that it is only by being engaged in the issues and the problems of our time, whether they affect us as individuals or not, that we can create a reality for that cherished but slightly tarnished abstraction known as "We the people."

# References

## Chapter One: In the Key of A: ALTRUISM

1. M. Udall, *Too Funny to be President,* Henry Holt and Company, New York, 1988.
2. H. Smith, *The Religions of Man,* Harper & Row, New York, 1958.
3. I. Goldman, *The Mouth of Heaven: An Introduction to Kwakiutl Religious Thought,* John Wiley & Sons, New York, 1975.

## Chapter Two: In the Key of B: BENEVOLENCE

1. M. R. MacDonald (adapted from), *Peace Tales: World Folktales to Talk About,* Linnet Books, Hamden, Connecticut, 1992.
2. Joel Oines, Personal correspondence, February 11, 1998.
3. A. Wolfe, *One Nation, After All: How the Middle Class Think about God, Country, and Family,* Viking Penguin, New York, 1998.
4. G. B. Shaw, *Pygmalion,* Penguin Books, London, 1957.
5. A. Schweitzer, *Memoirs of Childhood and Youth,* Macmillan Company, New York, 1949.

## Chapter Three: In the Key of C: COLLABORATION

1. S. B. Anthony, Woman Wants Bread, Not the Ballot! in *Feminism: The Essential Historical Writings,* M. Schneir (ed.), Vintage Books, New York, 1972.
2. G. Orwell, *1984,* Signet Classics, New York, 1961.
3. W. Wolfensberger, *The History of Human Services,* a presentation for Human Service Professionals at Madison, Wisconsin, 1982.
4. H. Lee, *To Kill a Mockingbird,* HarperCollins, New York, 1995.
5. E. Partridge, *A Concise Dictionary of Slang and Unconventional English,* P. Beale (ed.), Macmillan, New York, 1989.
6. W. Churchill, Crimes Against Humanity, in *Race, Gender and Class: An Anthology* (3rd Edition), M. Andersen and P. Collins (eds.), Wadsworth, Belmont, California, 1998.
7. A. M. Josephy, Jr., *500 Nations: An Illustrated History of North American Indians,* Alfred A. Knopf, New York, 1994.

8. H. W. Longfellow, The Song of Hiawatha, *Complete Poems,* Buccaneer Books, Cutchogue, New York, 1992.
9. R. Berkhofer, Jr., *The White Man's Indian: Images of the American Indian from Columbus to the Present,* Vintage Books, New York, 1979.
10. S. Terkel, *American Dreams: Lost and Found,* Ballantine Books, New York, 1980.

## Chapter Four:  In the Key of D:  DIVERSITY

1. J. Winegar, *Progress in Boston,* presented at the fifth annual conference of the Wisconsin State Human Relations Association, Milwaukee, Wisconsin, October 20, 1984.
2. G. K. Chesterton, *Charles Dickens, The Last of the Great Men,* The Readers Club, New York, 1942.
3. W. Shakespeare, Hamlet, in *William Shakespeare: The Complete Works,* A. Harbage (Gen. ed.), Penguin Books, Baltimore, Maryland, 1969.
4. H. Melville, *Moby-Dick or, The Whale,* Bobbs-Merrill, New York, 1964.
5. M. Gordon, *Assimilation in America: The Role of Race, Religion and National Origins,* Oxford University Press, New York, 1964.

## Chapter Five:  In the Key of E:  EMPATHY

1. N. Roden, *Life of Lord Byron,* Kennikat Press, Port Washington, New York, 1972.
2. C. A. MacKinnon, *Feminism Unmodified: Discourses on Life and Law,* Harard University Press, Cambridge, 1987.
3. K. Harbeck, *A Matter of Justice and Compassion,* presented at the Statewide Equity and Multicultural Education Conference, Milwaukee, Wisconsin, November 3, 1995.
4. L. Ferlinghetti, *A Coney Island of the Mind,* New Directions, New York, 1958.
5. M. Kantor, *Homophobia: Description, Development and Dynamics of Gay Bashing,* Praeger, West Point, Connecticut, 1998.
6. G. Doupe, True to Our Tradition, in *Homophobia: How We All Pay the Price,* W. Blumenfeld (ed.), Beacon Press, Boston, 1992.
7. J. Reinisch, *The Kinsey Institute New Report on Sex: What You Must Know to Be Sexually Literate,* St. Martin's Press, New York, 1990.

## Chapter Six:  In the Key of F:  FORGIVENESS

1. B. A. Cerf, *Try and Stop Me* (1944) included in *The Little, Brown Book of Anecdotes,* C. Fadiman (ed.), Little, Brown and Company, Boston, 1985.
2. M. L. King, Jr., *Strength to Love,* Fortress Press, Philadelphia, 1981.
3. S. Terkel, *Race: How Blacks and Whites Think and Feel about the American Obsession,* The New Press, New York, 1992.
4. J. Edwards, Sinners in the Hands of an Angry God, *Jonathan Edwards: Basic Writings,* Signet, New York, 1966.

5. *Holy Bible* (Revised Standard Version), Oxford University Press, New York, 1962. (Note: All Biblical references in this chapter are taken from this edition.)
6. *The Qur'an,* J. M. Rodwell (trans.), J. M. Dent & Sons, London, 1968. (Note: All references from the Qur'an in this chapter are taken from this translation.)
7. *Analects of Confucius,* A. Waley (trans.), Vintage Books, New York, 1938. (Note: All references to Confucius are taken from this translation.)
8. W. and A. Durant, *The Story of Civilization,* Simon & Schuster, New York, 1935.
9. B. Chatwin, *The Songlines,* Viking Penguin, New York, 1988.
10. H. Smith, *The Religions of Man,* Harper & Row, New York, 1958.
11. J. Swift, Thoughts on Various Subjects, *A Tale of a Tub with Other Early Works 1696-1707,* Basil Blackwell and Mott, Oxford, 1965.
12. E. Partridge, *Origins: A Short Etymological Dictionary of Modern English,* Greenwich House, New York, 1983.
13. A. J. Bahm, *The World's Living Religions,* Dell, New York, 1964.
14. J. Kozol, *The Night is Dark and I am Far From Home,* Bantam Books, New York, 1975.
15. N. Hawthorne, *Twice Told Tales and Other Short Stories,* Washington Square Press, New York, 1960.
16. e. e. cummings, *100 Selected Poems,* Grove Press, New York, 1959.
17. L. Tolstoy, *A Confession and What I Believe,* Oxford University Press, London, 1971.
18. W. Whitman, *Leaves of Grass,* Bantam Books, New York, 1983.

## Chapter Seven: In the Key of G: GRACE

1. L. Tolstoy (adapted from), Three Questions, in *Esarhaddon and Other Tales,* Books for Libraries Press, Freeport, New York, 1970.
2. J. Donne, Meditation 17 from *Devotions Upon Emergent Occasions,* in *Complete Poetry and Selected Prose of John Donne,* C. Coffin (ed.), The Modern Library, New York, 1952.
3. J. H. C. Newman, *Apologia Pro Vita Sua,* W. W. Norton & Company, New York, 1968.
4. M. Saunders, *Beautiful Joe,* Whitman, Racine, Wisconsin, 1955.
5. Saki (H. H. Munro), The Interlopers, in *The Short Stories of Saki,* Random House, New York, 1958.
6. J. D. Salinger, *The Catcher in the Rye,* Bantam Books, New York, 1964.
7. M. L. King, Jr., *Strength to Love,* Fortress Press, Philadelphia, Pennsylvania, 1981.
8. M. Twain, *Adventures of Huckleberry Finn,* Houghton Mifflin, Boston, 1958.
9. John 8:1-11, *Holy Bible* (Revised Standard Version), Oxford University Press, New York, 1962.
10. S. Terkel, *American Dreams: Lost and Found,* Ballantine Books, New York, 1980.

# Author Index

This index contains the names in alphabetical order of the people whose quotations appear in "Cross Talk" and in the "Hearing Voices" and "Echoes" sections of each chapter.

# General Index